FIRST TIME MOM & BABY SLEEP SOLUTION

2-in-1 Book

No Need to Panic, Pregnancy Guide to Be Ready for What is Coming in The Next 9 Months and Newborn Care + The Most Effective Baby Sleep Methods

FIRST TIME MOM SURVIVAL GUIDE

Don't Panic! We've Got Your Back. Be a Rockstar Mom & Prepare Every Step of The Most Exciting Journey of Your Life. Pregnancy, Labor, Childbirth and Newborn Baby Care

First Time Mom

Table of Contents

Introduction 7

Chapter 1: A Guide To First-Time Moms 9

Chapter 2: Things You Need to Consider When Preparing for Pregnancy 12

Chapter 3: Making it Through the Pregnancy 14

Chapter 4: First Trimester: What They Don't Tell You 25

Chapter 5: What To Expect During The Second Trimester 31

Chapter 6: What To Expect In Your Third Trimester 42

Chapter 7: Pregnancy Symptoms You Should Not Ignore 46

Chapter 8: Your Diet And Nutrition 56

Chapter 9: Your Diet And Common Health Issues 68

Chapter 10: Labor And Delivery 73

Chapter 11: What to Expect - Labor Induction 80

Chapter 12: What to Expect – Having a C-Section 84

Chapter 13: Preparing for Delivery 88

Chapter 14: What to Expect - Bringing Baby Home 91

Chapter 15: Tips for First Time Moms 96

Conclusion 107

First Time Mom
Introduction

Congratulations on purchasing this book.

The following chapters will discuss about every aspect of during and after the pregnancy: Expecting, Labor, Childbirth and Newborn. The information found in this book will best explore all you need to learn in order to experience a Healthy Pregnancy. It's your new mom's Survival Handbook.

Thanks again for choosing this audiobook! Every effort was made to ensure it is full of as much useful information as possible.

Please enjoy!

Every woman wants to fulfill her role of becoming a mother to her child. She dreams of carrying her unborn and giving birth to a healthy infant. There is something about first time pregnancy that makes it different and memorable. Nothing can compare to the excitement and anticipation of first time moms to conceive the bundle of her joy.

Along with the fervor of becoming a first time mom, you may feel a little confused, anxious, and fearful. The big responsibility of ensuring the good health and survival of the life inside your womb awaits you. To do so, you should prepare your body to give your unborn the healthy environment he/she needs to live.

It is easy to center your attention to the life inside your womb. You have to remember, though, that your unborn depends heavily on your own health and well-being. It is therefore essential that you have a body ready for pregnancy. Since this is your first time, you may need all the help you can get from your spouse, family, and friends.

First Time Mom

You will also find valuable resources online. This pregnancy guide intends to help you how to take good care of yourself for your baby from conception to childbirth. Written for first time moms, it covers everything you need to know in preparing your body before, during, and after your pregnancy. This is the ultimate baby care guide for first time moms like you.

Chapter 1: A Guide To First-Time Moms

So you want to be a good mom? Don't worry. You will be! You just need to know what to expect. This chapter is all about letting you know what you're in for –and while it's natural to be nervous about the whole thing, preparing for it will ensure that you and your baby will be healthy and happy.

First-time moms are in for a different kind of experience once a baby enters their life. It doesn't even start after delivery–it starts once you see those two pink lines confirming that you have a life in your womb. You'll experience a slew of emotions -- a mixture of excitement, happiness, fear, and many others. It's normal to be nervous. You'd even find yourself worrying a bit about pains during delivery. Aside from that, the imagination of a first-time mom usually goes into overdrive. You might find yourself thinking about the foreseeable future and worrying about whether you can give your baby a good life.

Emotions run high and you'll tend to be extra sensitive during pregnancy, thanks to hormones, which is why you really need to understand your needs and how your body works, and the changes that will occur–from the subtle to the not-so-subtle. If you do that, first-time pregnancy and parenting will be manageable.

The joys of pregnancy and parenthood are overwhelming, but pregnancies also come with a need for a great deal of work, patience, love, support, and understanding. Here are some of the challenges, reminders, and pieces of advice that you should consider so you will enjoy this new stage of your life.

What To Expect When You're Expecting

First Time Mom

Conception, pregnancy, childbirth, and child rearing are no walk in the park. It's easy to say you want to have a baby, but once the baby is there, you discover how hard reality bites. Here are some expectations you need to be ready for:

The Pains of Childcare

Childcare will definitely burn your energy especially the first few years, and more so, the first few months. You should be ready for sleep interruptions during the night. You will get exhausted during the day may not have enough energy to look after the baby at night. Once you're back to work, you have that to worry about too. You might want to consider asking for a more flexible shift at work. If that isn't possible, hire a nanny who can look after your child. It is going to be worth it. Nothing compares to the feeling of waking up and staying late just staring at the little angel.

Set Your Priorities

Once you're confirmed that a baby is on the way, it's time to readjust your priorities. This is the first thing you have to remember–you should not try to be a superwoman. You don't have to make sure that your house is spotless, that you serve well-planned healthy meals all the time, maintain your relationships with all friends and work full-time all while taking care of your baby. You have to be realistic about what can be done without stretching yourself too thin. Find out what's more important to you and build your schedule around that. Perhaps, you don't have to keep the place spotless. Perhaps, eating outa few nights a week is okay. You don't even have to completely stick to a rigid schedule. Part of being a parent is thinking on your feet.

Establish a support system

First Time Mom

You are going to be your child's anchor but it doesn't hurt to get support from other people, as well. Remember what they say about how it takes a village to raise a child. You don't need a literal village to help you out–you can just ask friends or family not exactly for help but for support. Ask someone over for dinner so you and your child can get some socialization with people other than each other. Also, contrary to popular belief, you can actually endear yourself to someone by asking for help–especially if it's something as easy as help with moving the couch. Even something as simple as calling your own parents to talk about how things are with your child is a good way to establish that support system.

Stay Healthy

Motherhood is going to take a lot of energy so staying fit is important. You should never forget to take care of yourself. That way, you can take care of your child and their needs. Motherhood is a 24/7 job, and you can't afford to get sick or fall to a serious condition because a tiny human being is now dependent on you. Still, you do need some time off to take care of your personal needs, which is why you'll need a readjustment of priorities and a decent support system.

It's challenging–but rewarding -- to be a first-time mom. There will be ups and downs, but if you are determined to take on the challenge, you'll find that it can be fun and exciting –even wondrous at times. Parenthood becomes even more meaningful once you start teaching your child the value of respect, love, and responsibility –and just how to be a good human being in general.

Chapter 2: Things You Need to Consider When Preparing for Pregnancy

When you get pregnant, your body goes through major changes. You might think that all the changes hormones brought during puberty were enough to make you crazy but just wait until they get to work during your pregnancy! Hence, it's crucial that prepare physically and also mentally. The physical aspect is a given, of course. After all, you'll be nourishing a life inside you. But you see, pregnancy is bound to catapult you into something you may not be quite prepared for. Yes, you expect to get pregnant someday and you might have even been fervently wishing for it. Whatever the case may be, expectation can be quite different from reality; thus, the need to prepare yourself mentally.

You may need to consider your career. This consideration goes hand-in-hand with finances, which is also a crucial part of being a parent. You'd want to make sure that your baby's needs are taken care of. There are some important questions that you will need to ask yourself. How quickly do you intend to get back to work? How do you manage your career and a baby? Pregnancy doesn't come free. In fact, it is expensive. Can you afford to leave your job and risk going through mental stress while trying to think of how you can make ends meet and sustain your pregnancy? Bear in mind the medical bills, the cost of having the baby, baby needs and supplies, and even your own needs. That's why it's important to prepare yourself mentally for the pregnancy challenge.

The next thing you need to work on is preparing your body for pregnancy. As mentioned in the beginning, your body will undergo changes before, during, and after the pregnancy. Therefore, it's important to make sure that your body stays healthy through the entire process. The first thing you need to do is to optimize your weight. You want to enter your pregnancy in the pink of health, so you need to ensure that you are neither overweight nor underweight. Start maintaining a healthy diet. Consult your obstetrician for help on this regard or ask her if she can refer you to a nutritionist. If you were a smoker, now's the best time to quit.

Smoking can lead to low birth weight for your baby, premature labor, and a plethora of other health problems for both you and the baby, not to mention that it can make conceiving a baby difficult in the first place because of the fertility problems it brings. Avoid cigarettes and secondhand smoke.

You may also prepare your body for the pregnancy by taking supplements and prenatal vitamins. Vitamins rich in folic acid and iron are vital, and you would do well to take these in large quantities once pregnant.

Chapter 3: Making it Through the Pregnancy

Keys to a Happy Healthy Pregnancy

It is ideal to start the lifestyle changes discussed in this chapter even before you become pregnant. But don't worry if you have not done it yet. You can always decide to adopt these changes as soon as you can.

Stay active.

Regular exercise will not only be good for you but for your growing baby, as well. It is important that you stick to a regular routine so you can ensure that your placenta grows big enough to supply oxygen and other nutrients to your baby. Regular exercise can also help keep your heart and your baby's heart in good condition. There have been many studies published to prove that women who remain active and exercise regularly have shorter, less painful deliveries.

Choose an activity that you find enjoyable. There is one basic principle you need to adhere to: always listen to your body. Don't do a particular exercise when it does not feel right. Don't attempt to beat your personal record or finish a marathon during your pregnancy.

Reduce toxins.

- Eat as much real and organic food as you can. Stay away from BPA and canned and processed foods.
- Stop using personal care products that include "parfum" or "fragrance" as ingredients. You can always choose products that have natural essential oils.

- Try making your own cleaning products or use natural ones such as castile soap, baking soda, essential oils and vinegar.

Eat whole foods.

It is ideal for you to eat a well-balanced diet that consists of sufficient amounts of vegetables, fruits, healthy fats and protein. Include a lot of leafy green vegetables in your diet because they are rich in vitamin B and folate, which reduces your baby's risks of neural tube defects.

Sufficient rest.

Your pregnant body needs sufficient sleep so that it will be able to revitalize itself from the higher demands of your growing baby. Even excessive worries and negative thoughts can drain you of physical energy. During the 1st trimester, you may have to sleep extra hours every day to allow your body to adjust to your pregnancy. Try taking a nap or a rest at any time in the day. Try to rest as much as you can.

Consider chiropractic care.

Getting chiropractic care during your entire pregnancy can remove interferences to your nervous system. It can relieve the tension in your back from carrying extra weight, as well as help in readjusting your posture. This can enhance the uterine function and overall development of your baby. It can also help balance your pelvis and remove unnecessary tension that is placed on your ligaments and muscles. Chiropractic care can also improve the positioning of your baby which can allow you to have better natural birth.

Educate yourself.

When you start announcing your pregnancy, a lot of people will start to give their unsolicited advice. They do not really mean harm but sometimes your family and friends can give you the wrong information. This is why it is very important that you perform your own research to see if any information, or any prescribed tests are truly necessary and if they have any side effects that you need to be aware of. Always keep in mind that you have the ultimate responsibility for your baby and every decision that is made is yours to make. Do not let anyone pressure you into something that you do not want to do, and do not feel guilty for your decisions.

Take dietary supplements.

Here are some of the dietary supplements you can consider taking during your pregnancy:

- Omega-3 which is important for the growth and development of your baby. It is also vital for the proper development of your baby's brain and nervous system. Make sure to ask your doctor which specific supplement is ideal for you to take.
- Vitamin D is important in reducing your risks of developing a lot of complications related to pregnancy, particularly gestational diabetes. Vitamin D is critical in the proper development of your baby's hormones, bones and muscles. It can also boost your own immune system while pregnant.
- Probiotics are important in helping your unborn baby obtain sufficient amounts of good bacteria that can help lower their risks of illnesses during the formative years.
- Folic acid allows the body to create new cells easier. During pregnancy, it can help increase the rate at which your baby develops. It can also help to ensure that your baby's lungs mature easier at the end of your pregnancy.
- DHA is important to your baby's brain development and it is important for establishing normal brain function. This is

a vitamin that is important during pregnancy, and essential for your baby after he is born.
- Iodine is a vitamin that is typically overlooked. Iodine is important for your baby's brain development during pregnancy and when you are breastfeeding. Since the type and amount of fish that you can eat is limited during this time, it is important that you seek it out elsewhere.

Prenatal Care

Prenatal care is extremely important to your unborn baby. This care allows your doctor to monitor what is going on with your baby while he is still in your tummy.

Prenatal care helps ensure that you and your baby remain as healthy as possible, and that any health conditions are taken care of in a timely manner. Your doctor will also be able to give you care advice that is customized to your individual needs, and what your baby needs.

Every woman, and her pregnancy is different. Even if you have been pregnant before, this pregnancy will be completely different. Therefore, you should treat this pregnancy as what it is, unique.

Most doctors recommend that you be seen in their office for prenatal care using the following schedule:

- Once a month for from the time you are one month pregnant until you are seven months pregnant.
  - Two times per month from the time you are seven months pregnant until you are eight months pregnant.
  - Every week from the time you are eight months pregnant, until you deliver.

First Time Mom

At your prenatal visits, your doctor will do several things, including a physical exam and order lab work.

You can expect the following things to happen at some point in your pregnancy:

- Check your blood pressure at every visit.
- Determine how much weight you have gained.
- Measure your belly to see how much baby has grown.
- Check your baby's heart rate.
- Determine whether you have a family history of disorders that may affect your pregnancy.
- A physical exam, including a pelvic exam.
- Blood based laboratory tests.
- Answer any questions you may have about your changing body.

How You Can Prepare for Doctor Visits

Over the next eight months, you and your doctor will become very close. Your doctor will be your go to person for questions and concerns that you have during your pregnancy. They are a great resource, but only if you handle this relationship in the right manner. Here is some amazing advice to ensure that you get the most out of this relationship.

Select the Right Doctor

By choosing the right doctor, you are doing you and your baby a huge favor. When getting your needed medical care you should take the step to create a solid relationship as doctor and patient. You should also make sure that you feel the doctor you choose to see is compassionate and competent. Mary Jane Minkin, MD says "Trust is one of the most important factors in a good doctor-patient relationship."

First Time Mom

Mary Jane Minkin is a clinical professor of gynecology and obstetrics at the School of Medicine at the Yale University. You and your doctor should be comfortable with each other. There should be no tension when he walks in the room or if you think he is mistreating you. If you think this is happening to you than you should try to find another midwife, doctor, or a new health care provider. You need to make sure that you find some one you click with and stay with them. Because there are so many legal issues there are a lot of doctors that are retiring from the field of obstetrics. This means that many of them have gone to being OB's.

Ask questions (within reason)

If this is your first time being pregnant than you no doubt have lots of questions. If you do than you most definitely should ask them. Just remember you only have so much time so try to ask a reasonable amount of questions. Make sure that you prioritize your most important questions so that you can ask a few at a time. This will make sure you get your most important questions answered first.

Write down your questions--and the answers

One of the most important things you can do when you have questions is to write them down in a notebook. This will make sure you don't forget what your questions were and you can take them with you to make sure you ask your doctor. You can also take your notebook with you so that when you ask your questions you can write down what the doctor has to say about it. This way you will have them with you all the time.

Tell your doctor at the start of your appointment that you have questions

Doctors have many preferences in when they like to ask you if you have any questions. Some will ask in the beginning or at the end. The ones that ask in the beginning of an appointment like to make sure that if it is something they need to check during the exam. You can also let them know in the beginning that there are things that you want to go over that might need checked during the exam.

Save late-night calls for emergencies

It is important to save questions that are not an emergency for your regular visits instead of taking up the doctors' time. Or you can call the office during business hours and ask questions.

Talk to the nurse

You can call your doctors office and talk to the nurse if you have any questions between appointments. There are some questions that nurses can answer immediately. This will keep you from having to wait on the doctor calling you back for an answer that the nurse could have given you. If the nurse can't answer your question they can arrange for the doctor to call you back.

Don't come spouting facts from the Internet

You can find some answers online. If you search the internet it helps to look for the websites that are legitimate medical sites. Also if you read something you should ask your doctor if what you read is true or not. You should not jump to conclusions from the internet and tell the doctor that what you read makes you think that you should have a C-section. Saying something like this can make your doctor become defensive and in turn making appointments intense.

Show that you're invested in your pregnancy

Here is one of the ways that you can help show your doctor that you really care and are going to invest time into your pregnancy. If you are a smoker and you choose to quit when you first find out that you are pregnant. This will allow the doctor to see that you truly care about the health of your baby and that your pregnancy goes more smoothly. This will make your life and the doctors life that much easier. The more effort you put into doing things right for your pregnancy the more the doctor will be willing to help you.

People will tell you throughout your pregnancy that you are glowing. It's true, you are. Pregnancy skin shines and you are beautiful. There are going to be times when you feel unbelievably womanly and graceful. You will feel like you could be Mother Earth herself. Truth time here. There are probably going to be more times that you feel like something the cat drug in. Pregnancy is hard. Truth time again. Morning sickness does not happen to everyone and some people barely get it. Some of you though are going to get it and get it bad. Holding down food, at least for the first few months, is going to be a memory for you.

Crackers do help. Ingesting a small handful of crackers before getting up out of bed in the morning can be a big help. It is important to eat small meals. If you start to feel like you are a little queasy or a little full then it is time to stop. You can always eat more later on! You are going to be thirsty when you are pregnant and it is very important for the sake of both you and the baby to stay well hydrated. However, when you have morning sickness do not guzzle water. If you drink too fast it is going to come back up. Just take small sips and you will have a much better chance to keep everything down.

Another good choice for morning sickness? Ginger! Some people drink ginger ale and some people take a ginger supplement. Another yummy way to do it is gingersnaps! They really do work but be careful not to scarf too many down at once. You don't want them coming back up!

For most pregnant women morning sickness does go away after the first three months. After that, if your sickness is gone, you may get very hungry! And yes, it is true, you will crave food. Cravings can be very hardcore! Don't be surprised if you burst into tears one day and cry your eyes out because the local mini mart is out of beef jerky or chocolate doughnuts. One month you may want nothing but steak lots of steak. Another month, meat may turn your stomach inside out and all you want to eat is cantaloupe. There is no rhyme or reason to it that's for sure!

Some foods you do need to avoid in pregnancy. You probably were not going to eat it anyway but no raw or undercooked meat. No rare steak for you girl! This does include fish so if you love sushi you will have to bid it farewell for a while. Oysters and clams are both a big no no. Eggs are ok but make sure to check that are pasteurized and cook them fully before eating. Truth time. No one likes to admit but a lot of people like raw cookie dough. In pregnancy though you are going to have to bake those cookies, raw cookie dough is definitely not allowed!

Your body and your mind is going to change. Having a child growing inside you is flat out amazing. Hearing the heartbeat for the first time is indescribable. You will feel emotions that you did not even know you were capable of having. A fierce protectiveness for the unborn child will seem to come out of nowhere. You will protect your stomach while out in public without even noticing you are doing it. One day you will feel a tiny flutter and wonder what if, this usually happens around month four, but the next flutter will be stronger and you will know without a doubt. It is your child in there moving and growing and kicking.

Your hair may look more lustrous and that is good because you are not allowed to dye it while you are pregnant. Your partner is most likely going to find you extremely sexy and believe it or not your sex drive is going to soar. If you were wondering, yes you can have sex while you are pregnant. You might even want to have a lot of it because the first few months after the baby is born are guaranteed to turn into a dry spell. If you experience any cramping or spotting after sex make sure to discuss this with your doctor. You are going to start to love your baby bump and continue to love it even as you grow. You will sing to your baby and people will say hello to the little one through your belly button. (Whether or not you want them to!) These changes are truly amazing!

Truth time. Not all the changes can be classified as amazing, in fact some or downright annoying and uncomfortable. Heartburn you should expect. Mothers that have never had heartburn will start to have it. Anything can cause it too, even sugar! It is unpleasant. Small meals and sleeping on pillows (so you aren't lying flat) can make a huge difference. Your boobs are going to get bigger, possibly a lot bigger! Yes, this can be nice. However, you will probably be surprised to see your nipples leaking. Months before your milk comes in, your colostrum can start to leak, this is normal! Colostrum is the thick creamy nourishment your baby will drink for the first few days of her life. So, if you see some leakage from your nipples, do not fear! If it worries you then calling your doctor is always a viable option.

In fact, do not forget that is why your doctor is there! Call their office anytime day or night when you are worried about something. It is their job to take care of you!

The more your baby grows the more your body stretches. Babies are so small you wouldn't think that your body would stretch too much, right? Wrong! The ligaments that run from your naval up to your ribs are going to hurt and at times they are going to hurt very badly. Getting off your feet whenever possible is always a smart decision. The longer you stand the more you are going to feel the stretch. There are products out there you can take advantage of. A belly belt is kind of like a girdle only it holds your baby up instead of your stomach in. The choice to use one of these is completely up to you.

First Time Mom

Most likely you will find yourself unconsciously holding your baby up long before you deliver him. The tiny precious feet you are so looking forward to kissing or going to feel monstrous when they are in your ribs. Not only do all babies like to move and kick but they have some sort of sixth sense about kicking mommy directly in the ribs or jumping up and down on mama's bladder.

Speaking of bladders. Truth time again. There is a good chance you may pee your pants at some point. At the very least trickle. The last couple months of pregnancy the baby is growing rapidly towards full term size. Your internal organs fit inside you quite nicely before you got pregnant. Do they go anywhere when you are pregnant? Oh no! They just get squished! One day when you are nine months pregnant you are going to cough and see just how squished your bladder really is!

Sleep may be difficult, especially near the end. If you were a belly sleeper before you have some adjusting to do. Have you ever tried to sleep on your stomach with a beach ball underneath you? It just does not work. Anytime you can rest though take full advantage of it. Labor and delivery is coming and your body needs to be ready to handle it.

Chapter 4: First Trimester: What They Don't Tell You

The first trimester of pregnancy is really an introduction period for your body and the new baby. Much is going on inside you and changes are happening to make room for the baby to grow. And get all of the nutrients it needs to mature into a full term fetus. The first trimester is the moment of conception up to the 12th week, or the 3rd month. For many women this is the most difficult trimester of them all. Your body is making a lot of adjustments.

The experience during first trimester varies for all women. You may not feel pregnant or then again you may feel very pregnant. Some women say that they have a full feeling inside of their stomachs from the very moment they conceive. Others even swear they know the exact moment that the baby was conceived. While there are no medical tests that can confirm a pregnancy this early, it is very much possible for a woman to have this type of experience.

It is hard to know for sure what you will experience or how intense your experience will be. Heartburn, morning sickness, being uncomfortable and nauseated -- these are all things that are commonly experienced by pregnant women during the first trimester.

What is the truth of the matter? Sometimes these experiences can be very difficult, and even if you have experienced them before pregnancy, these experiences are more intense during pregnancy. Heartburn is maximized 10 times over; your body is hot and you feel bloated. Even the smell of water makes you want to run to the bathroom to vomit. Morning sickness, even when you do not actually vomit, can cause pure misery. And, has anyone warned you about dry heaves? These are a few of the common experiences that occur during your first trimester.

Morning Sickness & More

Morning sickness should really have a new name because it is very misleading. It is sickness all right, but it does not discriminate and it causes trouble in more than just the morning. For some pregnant women morning sickness can be absolutely horrible, disrupting life in every single way. These women cannot stay out of the bathroom, and sometimes it is not that they are throwing up, but that they feel as if they want to 24 hours a day. It is not a pretty picture that we are painting here, and that is because there is nothing pretty about morning sickness. It can occur morning, noon and night, and sometimes it occurs during all three and never goes away. A package of saltines on hand to bite on when morning sickness strikes is the new-mom secret. A Sprite or ginger ale can also do the trick to ease your sickness. Do not think that you will only have mild nausea in the morning and it will all go away. This is one of the marks of pregnancy and most women will have it. And, chances are that it is going to be pretty severe for the first trimester. If you do not experience morning sickness, or if it is something that you experience only in mild form, then you are very lucky.

If you normally do not go to the bathroom very often, then get ready for that to change after pregnancy. The bathroom is your best friend during your pregnancy. Going there will be something that you have to do often! As soon as you wash your hands and get comfortable on the couch, you will have to go again. There's a lot of pressure with a baby sitting on your bladder, even if it does only weigh a half an ounce. The problem with frequent urination is that it doesn't go away until the pregnancy is over. In fact, the bigger baby gets, the worse the problem gets, too.

Heartburn, Acne & More

Heartburn is also something that you probably will experience during the first trimester. It is one of the most common side effects during pregnancy. Women who are pregnant with multiples report that the heartburn is even worse. However, most women with child will experience heartburn, and it really burns. It is a good idea to go ahead and get a bottle of Tums and expect to chew them like candy. You can drink water to help ease heartburn as well.

Even if you have been lucky enough to have never had a pimple before in your life, the hormonal changes with pregnancy may very well bring on an outbreak. For many women in their first trimester acne is a big concern. Many pregnant women fear using the products sold over the counter to get rid acne, scared that it will harm the baby. However, there are numerous home remedies for acne available that are perfectly safe for both mom and baby, while also being effective at eliminating acne breakouts. Some women experience no breakouts, some a few pimples and zits, and other women have full blown breakouts, and again, this is not something that anyone can determine ahead of time. If it does affect you, the key is to be prepared and ready to treat. If you do want to help keep your skin looking its very best, make sure that you wash the face twice per day, using a gentle soap or a mild cleanser. Follow up with a moisturizer to keep the skin soft. You can also talk to your doctor about acne treatments if you do not want to use those that are sold over the counter. Your doctor can give you many other tips and tricks to help combat acne as well.

You are going to be tired. Really tired. No matter how much you sleep it will never seem as if you have had enough. And, when you are awake you are probably not going to be jumping up and down and full of energy. Pregnancy takes a lot out of you. Make plans to settle down just a little bit, compared to your normal activities, that is. While you do not have to sit in the house and do nothing but protect your belly all day, you do need to make a few exceptions, avoid a few things and prepare for those days when staying in bed. You are not going to be getting a lot of sleep in nine months, and you are going to want it. So, go ahead and take advantage of it now, and sleep in when you can and put some of the normal activities to the side. The most important things that you can do right now is take care of your body and the new baby that is growing inside of you, and one of the things that you can do is get the extra sleep that you need.

An Emotional Roller Coaster

Aside from those kinds of changes, expect your emotions to be up and down. Many would suspect you were bipolar if they did not know you were pregnant. The smallest of things can cause an emotional meltdown -- and we do mean a meltdown. Uncontrollable crying isn't uncommon, and expect to be ultra-sensitive. You may cry over every single movie that you see, and something as crazy as getting a hamburger with a pickle on it can send you into frenzy. Your body is going through many changes. It isn't your fault; it is all of those hormones that your body is accumulating.

Mood changes are very common. One minute you are fine and the next you are not. It is just a part of pregnancy. This is first seen in the first trimester, but it is one of those things that continue throughout the entire pregnancy.

Here are a few other very important things that you need to know about pregnancy in the first trimester.

1. You will also worry about everything. What if you fall while walking down the street? What if something is wrong with the baby? Are you going to be a good mother? Will you produce enough breast milk? What are the best diapers? While seemingly irrational to the non-pregnant brain, prepare to worry about the smallest, sillier of things as if they were a major life decision. Just remember, this too

shall pass. It is not uncommon for pregnant women to worry about everything. It is a new experience and there is a lot that is going on inside of your body, after all.

2. During the first trimester you might also notice veins in your body that you have never noticed before. This is not uncommon and many women experience this. Whether in your arms or legs, veins seem to pop out of nowhere.

3. Noticing that your legs are a little hairier than they usually are, or that your hair is back the day after you shave? Again this is something that you should plan for and prepare for, because for most pregnant women it happens. Pregnancy is one of the healthiest times in the world, as long as you take care of yourself, and this means that hair (everywhere on the body) is growing rapidly. The hair on top of your head will also have this same effect. If you have thin hair, ordinarily expect to get a totally new mane that you will absolute love.

Your Doctor Visits

There is little change that comes during the first trimester physically, and chances are that most people will not even realize that you are pregnant. Although they say that you cannot feel baby move around until many weeks into the pregnancy, it is very much possible to feel butterflies in the stomach, which is the baby. This is just something that you know when you feel it. It is certainly a feeling like nothing else in this world.

The doctor will see you once a month during the first trimester, and sometime during the 8th week he will listen for a heartbeat. This is an amazing sound to hear. Some doctors will record it for you if you would like, and this is definitely an amazing memory to have to hold. Your doctor will also give you a due date, a date of conception and a ton of information to take home with you and read, including pregnancy magazines.

Most moms would tell you to read these books and learn as much as you can, and you should. But, at the same time, remember that you need to give yourself leeway and rarely does a pregnancy happen just as they predict in those magazines. Every woman will have her own unique experience and this is all a part of the enjoyment of being pregnant. Learn from the books and magazines and do all that you can to abide by the rules and the tips that they offer. But at the same time, do not make the mistake of thinking that everything is going to happen just like it says in those books.

And, another tip, do not throw all of those advertisements away. You are still new to being pregnant, and you are still unaware of just what it means to be a new mom. But, the pregnancy companies out there do and they are ready to help you out. Baby will drink a massive amount of formula, and at a cost of about $30 a can, this can get expensive quickly. Add to that the cost of diapers and you have a very expensive new life forming inside of you. It is all worth it, but you might as well take advantage of all of the help that you can get. Many of those advertisements that you see in magazines are for baby clubs. It is a good idea to go ahead and join them now. You will get plenty of full size products in the mail and lots of extra goodies, too. This can include diaper bags, bottles, wipes, formula, birth announcements, photos and more. You never know what kind of offers that you will find inside, but join all of the clubs that you can!

Chapter 5: What To Expect During The Second Trimester

Week 13

This is the onset of the second trimester, and your baby is now at 7.5cm in length and 25 grams in weight, which is actually the size of a peach. The skeletal part of your baby's body begins to develop starting with the collar (clavicle) and thigh (femur) bones. Also, your baby starts to turn its head, swallow and hiccup. The baby can also kick their legs. The baby's stomach and vocal cord start to develop at the 13th week. In addition, your baby starts to take his first breath. The blood from the umbilical cord supplies the oxygen, and with a closer look it will seem as though your baby is breathing under water.

For you, you should be back to your normal self with minimal episodes of morning sickness, and the good news is that your chances of having a miscarriage is now a low probability. Also, you should notice a little more expansion of your waistline and bust.

Week 14

Your baby is becoming bigger and stronger at this stage. The arms are fully grown in proportion to the rest of the body while the legs are still undergoing growth. The baby's length is 8cm (about half a banana) while the current weight should be around 42 grams. The baby has hair and the eyebrows are formed before the end of this week. One surprising development process that occurs at this stage is the development of your baby's fingerprints. The baby will also start sucking their thumb. Also, your baby will start making use of their facial muscles to make expressions like squinting, frowning and grimacing.

You may suffer occasional forgetfulness as a result of the pregnancy hormones in your body. Also, nose bleeding is to be expected at this stage and you will experience a huge craving for food.

Week 15

Remember that I mentioned earlier that the baby's head was a third of its entire body. The good news is that by this fifteenth week, your baby's head must have grown into proportion with the rest of the body. The baby is 11.5cm (about the size of an orange) long, and his ears are fully developed at this stage to hear sounds. The baby will also grow some fine downy hair referred to as lanugo meant to keep the baby warm until they are able to develop a layer of subcutaneous fat to keep them warm after birth. The baby's sucking, swallowing and gasping skills have also advanced and will probably have developed their taste buds. The baby can also hear your voice by now so you should try to sing to them or talk to them often.

Although your baby's eyelids should still be closed at the moment, he can recognize lights. For instance, if you put a flashlight directly on your belly, you will feel some movements; that is your baby moving away from the light.

You will notice a dark line from your navel and down your abdomen and your baby bump starts getting noticeable.

Week 16

Your baby is probably the size of an avocado. At this stage, your baby's joints and limbs should be fully developed. Their backbone is also a lot stronger and they have probably mastered the art of sucking the thumb. Also, your baby's nervous system starts to connect with other muscles that will help your baby's movements. I talked about your baby developing skin much earlier. The skin at this stage is so transparent that you can clearly see the tiny veins underneath the skin. Their facial muscles are also a lot more developed so their expressions are a lot more visible although the baby doesn't yet know how to control them. The baby will also develop the ability to grab and play with the umbilical cord.

Your libido increases considerably. You will find yourself feeling the urge to have sex more often than usual. You can have as much sex as you want at this period without harming your baby. All you need to do is to find a comfortable sex position since your bump might get in the way.

Week 17

Your baby weighs around 150g in this week, and his or her facial features are fully developed. You may start feeling some firm movements in your womb. Your baby's brain begins to regulate the heartbeat to 140 to 150 beats per minute, which is still twice your own heartbeat. Meanwhile, your baby's fingerprints become more pronounced at this stage.

You will start feeling more energetic and less tired than you have in the past weeks. Now is the time to make use of that energy. Get the baby's room ready, take a workout class for pregnant mothers or join a walking group. Get out there and put that energy to good use! Getting more physically active now will help greatly later on, trust me!

Week 18

Your baby at this stage has grown to 14cm, and weighs almost 200g. The eggs start developing (in a female child), while the nerves begin to build up a protective covering referred to as myelin to enable the nervous system to develop and function properly upon birth. The baby at this period has also been engaged in lots of movements including kicking, tumbling and rolling. Their grip is also developed. The baby is also able to hold their umbilical cord firmly when playing.

Meanwhile, you tend to add more weight as the days go by. This is a combination of your weight, your baby's weight, the amniotic fluid, and the placenta.

Week 19

Your baby weighs about 240g and is about 14cm long at this stage. The baby's weight is more than that of the placenta now. Your baby's legs have grown into proportion with the rest of his body while the cartilage continues to harden. The baby's skin becomes less translucent and the skin pigments, which will determine the color of your baby's skin, will start to form. The baby will also start developing the Vernix Caseosa (this is the waxy or cheese-like white substance that coats your baby's skin when he or she is born) on its body to protect its body from the side effects of his contact with amniotic acid. The baby will also start developing some hair on its scalp, although the hair at this stage will be white and pigment free since the baby's hair color is yet to be determined. The baby can hear you well at this time.

You will notice a considerable increase in your bump size. Also heartburn and indigestion will be some of the symptoms that may occur during this period.

Week 20

Your baby is entering his fifth month this week. He or she will grow stronger and bigger to 16.5 cm length size; about the size of a banana but growing pretty fast. Also, at this stage, the part of the brain that controls the senses will start developing to help your baby to taste, see, touch and smell.

Your baby will also start producing something referred to as Meconium, within their bowel. Meconium refers to a harmless mixture of the amniotic fluid, which the baby has swallowed already, coupled with dead skin cells and digestive secretions. This mixture forms the baby's first bowel movement just after birth.

Your back may start aching as your bump continues to get bigger. Also, you may experience pain in your pelvis at this stage in your pregnancy as well.

Week 21

This week, your baby has increased in length to make him or her about 27cm long and weighing about 360g. Although your baby continues to add weight, it still lacks fats in its body. However, they will start adding on some fats that will ultimately give them the chubby 'baby' look when you first see them. The eyebrows have also developed and the eyelids can actually blink at this time.

One good point at this stage is that your baby's taste buds are fully developed to enable them to taste different flavors from the food you eat as they swallow the amniotic fluid. Also, the vernix caseosa is fully developed right now.

You should be making frequent visits to the antenatal ward by now. Antenatal classes help you (and your partner) prepare for labor, birth and early parenthood. You might also be interested in breastfeeding workshops as well.

Week 22

First Time Mom

The baby is now about the size of a papaya, about 27cm from head to toe and still growing fast. The body will also keep growing its placenta to provide nourishment for the baby.

The baby at this stage gets his nourishment from the placenta instead of the yolk sac, and his or her gums and tooth bud are in place now. Although your baby's eyes are fully developed, the eyes have no color because of the absence of the pigment in their iris. Your baby has now mapped a sleeping and waking up time for themselves and the pancreas is intact now.

Your major problem at this stage will be your swollen feet and ankles as your baby belly becomes bigger.

Week 23

Your baby looks more like a newborn baby but just smaller. It is now 30cm long and weighs 500g, and its body at this stage has started producing fats, so it will start bulking up from this week. When the baby is very active, you should be able to see him or her moving under your skin. The skin is still translucent such that you can see the bones and organs through the skin. At this age, the baby won't jump as much when exposed to loud noises. You can start playing classical music to sooth them.

You will continue to notice a considerable weight gain in your baby, which is also manifested in your own weight gain.

Week 24

Your baby is 1 foot long, and weighs 600g. Medically, it has been proven that a baby born at this stage (that is prematurely) has a high survival rate. Your baby can detect the sound of your heartbeat and your voice at this stage while his or her eyebrows and hair are fully developed now. Additionally, the baby's lungs have grown such that it can now breathe in actual air rather than fluids (thanks to the production of surfactant. If the baby doesn't produce this substance, it will have some breathing problems) and their face has nicely developed eyebrows, eyelashes and hair, which is still white (lacking pigmentation).

You may experience bleeding in your gums around this time, which is one dental problem that is synonymous with pregnancy.

Week 25

The baby at this time is growing fast. He or she gets to the size of 13 ½ inches long and with a weight of about 1 ½ pounds. The baby also starts plumping up thanks to the buildup of fat deposits under the skin to make them look more like normal. The baby will probably be hyperactive at this period (with such activities like somersaults, and wriggling). They will also be responsive to certain sounds so singing to them wouldn't be a bad idea.

Week 26

Your baby has grown to 2lbs and 35.5cm long, and the eyes are finally open. There is an increase in your baby's brain activity during this period and the testicles (if it is a boy) are descending to his scrotum (this takes 2-3 months to complete). You will probably start experiencing some more contractions, which are similar to menstrual cramps coupled with pain as the developing fetus stretches the uterus. The baby's circulatory system is well developed while the umbilical cord keeps on thickening as it gets stronger to support the supply of various nutrients to the baby.

Week 27

Your baby's weight is at 875g now and his eyesight has developed well enough to differentiate between night and day, but that doesn't mean that your baby will keep to the rule of sleeping in the night. Also, your baby's brain is in the final stage of development now. The baby also hiccups often and will probably do that more often when you eat spicy foods.

Your appetite is likely to increase and you will have cravings for food you don't typically eat as part of your normal diet. Like the famous pickles and ice cream combo.

Tips To Survive The Second Trimester

Backache

There is extra pressure on your back from carrying your baby. You can ease it off a bit by always using a chair with back support, sleep on your side with a pillow in between your legs and avoid picking heavy items off the ground.

Nosebleeds

The mucous membrane in your nose is swollen because of the hormonal changes taking place in your body, which may lead to constant nosebleeds for you. You need to keep your head up and apply gentle pressure to your nose to stop the bleeding.

Appearance Of Varicose Veins

They appear as a result of an increase in circulation of blood in your body to send blood to the growing fetus. The veins will disappear with time after birth.

Weight Gain

After your morning sickness subsides, your appetite returns in full force. You are likely to gain 1 to 3 pounds every week during this time. You have to work on practicing portion control for whatever you eat.

Nutrition

Vital organs of the body are beginning to develop. As such, you have to continue with foods high in protein and vegetables. Eat more of fiber-filled food to keep you full.

Exercise

With the stop in morning sickness and the regaining of your strength, you can start mild workout regimes, yoga, and meditation to keep fit.

Braxton Hick's Contraction

This is also known as fake contraction, and occurs towards and during the later part of the third trimester. The Braxton hick is a warm up exercise to prepare your uterus for labor. There is nothing much you can do about the fake labor but if it becomes so intense, then you may need to visit the hospital. At this time, you can probably sense some metallic taste in your mouth due to toxins accumulation from the lymphatic system. Don't worry; it will improve with time.

Colostrum leakage

Besides having tender breasts, you will probably start producing colostrum (a liquid from the breasts, which is often clear or creamy yellow with the consistency of syrup) from the 14th to the 16th week. If you notice some blood here, this is probably due to the rapid growth of blood vessels growing in the ductal system as your body preps for breastfeeding. Use breast pads inside your bra to deal with this.

Skin changes

Your skin, hair, and nails might start having changes like pigmentation, stretch marks, red spider veins, hormonal rashes, dry and oily skin, skin tags etc. Worry not because this is completely normal.

Swelling and fluid retention

This is referred to as edema (this starts at around 20 weeks into the pregnancy). You may also notice swellings on your hands, legs, and feet; these often become worse when it is hot. Varicose veins are usually linked to causing swelling. You should try to get your blood pressure tested if your swelling doesn't go away after week 20.

Gestational hypertension

This might happen when you are around 20 weeks pregnant. And if you have gestational hypertension coupled with high protein levels in your urine, you might be suffering from preeclampsia, which is usually characterized with kidney problems, visual changes and headaches.

Note: Having gestational hypertension is likely to make you increase your risk of stillbirth, intrauterine growth restriction, preterm birth, and placental abruption. Get your weight under control because this is closely linked to gestational hypertension.

Gestational diabetes

Ensure to have your blood sugar tested just to help you determine whether you might be having gestational diabetes since suffering from this could put you and the baby at risk. Weight and your diet are key determinants of this. Therefore, making some necessary changes to your diet could minimize your chances of developing such problems.

First Time Mom

You will also need to deal with rapid weight gain, weird dreams, itchy breasts, sleeping problems, increased libido and energy, leg cramps, itchy bumps, heartburn, backache and others. These shouldn't be any problem, as they will pass with time.

Chapter 6: What To Expect In Your Third Trimester

The third trimester is the final trimester of your actual pregnancy! While many believe that pregnancy will continue into a fourth trimester, or your postpartum period, your physical pregnancy will be done by the end of this trimester! That is, you will be giving birth to your baby! This final trimester brings a whole new myriad of symptoms, if you didn't already guess that, but at the same time after all of this practice, you are probably more than ready to manage them!

During the third trimester, you are going to want to be extra cautious of your body, because this is when labor will happen! For some women, labor happens on or after their due date, but for others they can go into early labor. It is important that you stay in tune with your body so you can alert your doctor if any major changes occur. In this chapter, you will learn what normal symptoms are, and what you should look out for! As well, you will learn more about what to expect with your doctors' visits.

SYMPTOMS

The symptoms you will experience in the third trimester are different, but not terribly different, from those you have already experienced. For the most part, they will simply be exaggerated versions of the symptoms you've already been experiencing. However, there are a few additional ones you might experience. You can learn all about it below!

LEG PAINS

This trimester, you are going to continue to experience the leg pains you have already likely been experiencing throughout the second trimester. The larger you get, the more pressure it puts on your legs and it can become very painful. Luckily, these will go away once your baby is born! In the meantime, you should do your best to stay off of your feet for long periods of time. You can also drink coconut milk or eat bananas, which are both rich in potassium, a nutrient that can significantly help reduce leg cramping.

NECK AND SHOULDER PAIN

Your growing belly is putting a lot of forward pressure on your back, which can also affect your neck and shoulders. You may notice your neck and shoulders are feeling just as bad as your lower back feels. This is completely normal. The best thing you can do is take a warm bath (but not hot!), get gentle massages, and relax a lot. If you find that it is affecting your sleep, try using body pillows and other pillows to help you support your back, legs, and belly.

HUNGRY, BUT NOT

A symptom many women report feeling that is extremely uncomfortable is the feeling that they are incredibly hungry, but are not able to eat. This is because your body needs more nutrition in order to support the growing baby. However, because your baby is getting so big, your stomach is running out of room! That means you don't have to eat as much to feel incredibly full. The best way to combat this symptom is to eat high-protein and nutrient rich mini-meals several times throughout the day. This will help keep you full and give your body all of the nutrients it needs without feeling excessively full.

LACK OF BLADDER CONTROL

Many people experience lack of bladder control when they are in their late pregnancy stages. The best thing to do is stay near a washroom, and relieve your bladder regularly. You may also wish to wear a pad if you will be going out, as they help to keep you from accidentally peeing your pants. As well, you may wish to lean forward when you are peeing to help get all of the urine out of your bladder, as the pressure of your baby may prevent you from eliminating your bladder completely.

CONSTIPATION

While your urine may be hard to stop, your bowels may slow down all on their own. This is caused, again, by all of the pressures and hormones going on in your body. You can combat this symptom through eating dates, prunes, and other fiber-rich foods that can help keep things flowing. As well, make sure you're staying hydrated, as that is important for you and your body, and it will help keep things moving.

DOCTOR VISITS AND MEDICAL TESTS

Your third trimester is going to be the most intensive one you will experience in regards to doctors' appointments. Towards the end of your third trimester, you are going to have your doctor visits increase to weekly visits. The exact time this will happen will depend on your doctor, the healthiness of your pregnancy, and whether or not you have been showing any signs of labor.

The doctors' appointments in this trimester will continue to include all of the same things as previous ones did: they will weigh you, measure your abdomen, check your blood pressure and pulse, and take a urine sample to check for protein in the urine. Towards the end of the trimester, you will likely also get pelvic exams to see if your cervix is dilating at all. At the end of each appointment, you will be informed of what to look for in the coming days.

First Time Mom

You actually won't experience any medical examinations this trimester, unless you are carrying an at-risk pregnancy. If you have high or low blood pressure, gestational diabetes, or any other pregnancy ailment, your doctor may require you to get an ultrasound or blood test taken to monitor your pregnancy a little more closely. Otherwise, you will not experience any further medical tests!

Chapter 7: Pregnancy Symptoms You Should Not Ignore

For many women, the third trimester goes all the way through effortlessly. For others, particularly those who are carrying at-risk pregnancies, you might run into a few complications. While your doctor has likely discussed this with you, particularly if you are known to be a high risk pregnancy, it can still be good to have this knowledge on hand. The following symptoms are things you should never avoid during your pregnancy. If any of these occur, you should call your doctor immediately or head to the maternity ward at your hospital.

EXCESSIVE PAIN ANYWHERE IN YOUR BELLY

Experiencing aches and pains is completely normal during pregnancy, especially in the third trimester. As your baby grows more and more, he or she will be running out of room and you may experience pain due to your baby's movement. However, if you are experiencing severe pain that is not related to the baby moving around, regardless of where it is in your stomach, you should call your doctor right away. You should be sure to monitor it especially if this pain persists or won't go away no matter what you do.

A HIGH FEVER WITH NO SYMPTOMS

If you have an extremely high fever but aren't experiencing symptoms of the flu, you should contact your doctor right away. This is not a common symptom late in pregnancy, and could indicate that you are presently fighting an infection. Your doctor will be able to help you confirm an accurate diagnosis and help reduce your fever depending on what he or she discovers.

EXCESSIVE VISUAL DISTURBANCES

While a slight change in vision is normal during pregnancy, excessive visual disturbances are not. If you are experiencing double vision, blurred vision, dimming or flashing spots, or other lights that are lasting for more than two hours or that are making you feel unwell, you should call your doctor right away. These symptoms are not normal and should be addressed immediately.

EXTREME SWELLING IN HANDS AND FEET

Swelling due to increased blood volume and fluid retention is normal, but extreme or excessive swelling in your hands and feet are not. If these symptoms appear suddenly or are accompanied by a headache or problems with your vision, you should contact your doctor.

SEVERE HEADACHE THAT WON'T GO AWAY

If you are experiencing a sudden and bad headache that won't go away after two to three hours, you should contact your doctor. If you are experiencing a headache alongside excessive swelling or visual disturbances, you should call your doctor right away and get seen as soon as possible.

ANY AMOUNT OF VAGINAL BLEEDING

When labor is about to start, you may experience something called a bloody show. However, if you experience bleeding that is heavy, light, dark, or otherwise abnormal, you should contact your doctor. In the earlier stages of pregnancy, light spotting is usually just implantation bleeding. However, any time after implantation, any amount of blood may be a concern. You should also look out for other symptoms, such as abdominal pain or back pain, which can be a potential sign of miscarriage.

FLUIDS LEAKING FROM YOUR VAGINA

It is really common for you to experience an increase in cervical discharge, as your body is working harder to keep potential bacteria build up out of your body to prevent infections. However, if you notice a watery fluid leaking from your vagina before 37 weeks, you will need to call your doctor right away. They will likely want to admit you to the hospital to check on your membranes and make sure they haven't ruptured. If they have, they will need to treat you to help prevent infection and prepare you and your baby for a potential premature labor and birth.

A SUDDEN AND DRAMATIC INCREASE IN THIRST, WITH REDUCED URINATION

Pregnant women are at risk for dehydration, so it is important that you are drinking a lot of water throughout your entire pregnancy. However, if you notice that you are suddenly starting to feel extremely thirsty, and you aren't urinating as often, you will want to talk to your doctor. This can be a symptom of dehydration, or it can be a symptom of gestational diabetes. Your doctor is the only person who can determine the exact cause, so you will need to speak with them to get assistance.

URINARY TRACT INFECTION SYMPTOMS

Urinary tract infections can be particularly dangerous during pregnancy, so you will want to discuss any UTI symptoms you may experience with your doctor. They will treat you and help ensure that the infection does not affect your uterus or your growing baby.

SEVERE OR EXCESSIVE VOMITING

Vomiting has the ability to cause dehydration and weakness in anyone, but especially a pregnant mother. While vomiting itself doesn't necessarily indicate anything is wrong, and it won't hurt your baby, you should make sure you keep your doctor in the loop about this. This will help them monitor you and ensure you aren't becoming severely dehydrated. If you are vomiting too much, you may need to be admitted to the hospital to receive fluids in order to keep you hydrated.

If you are later in your pregnancy and start suddenly vomiting an excessive amount, especially with a pain just below the ribs, you should call your doctor right away. This can be a symptom of a few different complications, all of which will need to be treated by a doctor.

FAINTING OR DIZZINESS

If you haven't eaten enough during the day, you may experience fainting or dizziness. However, it can also be caused by low blood pressure. It is important that you contact your doctor about this symptom if it is persistent, or if you faint at all. They will want to make sure that you are well, and work with you to prevent it from happening again.

SLOWED DOWN FETAL MOVEMENTS

Most often, your doctor will ask you to monitor fetal movements, to ensure your baby is moving regularly. If at any time you realize you have not felt your baby move in a while, or you perform a kick count and your baby is not as active as normal, you will want to contact your doctor. In most cases, this simply means the baby is resting. However, in some extreme cases, this can be a problem that needs to be addressed immediately.

OVERALL ITCHING, SEVERE ITCHINESS

First Time Mom

When you are pregnant, you are likely to experience itchiness in your belly and back area as your skin stretches and grows to accommodate for the growing baby. However, if you are noticing that your entire body is extremely itchy, particularly in your palms and the soles of your feet, you should call your doctor.

SYMPTOMS OF JAUNDICE

Any symptoms of jaundice need to be immediately addressed by your doctor. This can include: yellowed skin or eyes, dark urine, and pale stools. If you have any of these symptoms, you need to talk to your doctor immediately as they will want to have you admitted to the hospital for treatment. Jaundice is caused by an underactive or infected liver, and this needs to be addressed immediately.

IF YOU FALL OR EXPERIENCE A TRAUMA TO YOUR BELLY

If at any time in your pregnancy you fall or experience some kind of trauma to your belly, such as it being hit by something, you need to visit your doctor. While your belly will be fairly resilient, it is still important that you doctor ensures nothing has impacted the baby in a bad way. You should call your doctor immediately after a fall or blow to your belly to get help.

IF SOMETHING JUST "FEELS" EXTREMELY WRONG

Some women do not have an exact symptom of anything wrong, they simply feel extremely wrong. If you think something is not right with your body, baby, or pregnancy overall, you should talk to your doctor. They will look over your vital signs and ensure everything is wrong. While in many instances this can arise from anxiety, in some cases this feeling can indicate something is wrong, despite no symptoms really being present. Always trust your intuition!

More Pregnancy Secrets No One Tells You

First Time Mom

We hope that you have gained a lot of information that you did not already know about your pregnancy and are now preparing adequately. Pregnancy is an amazing journey, and, when you know everything that is probably going to happen, it can be an even easier journey for you to make. However, we are still not done and there are a lot of other pregnancy secrets that no one ever seems to tell you but you still must know. If you want to know the rest of those secrets, keep reading.

Touchy Feely Kind of World

It is up to you as to how you will react, but go ahead and start planning it now: People are going to touch your belly. Yes, you can expect all of your family and your friends to do it, and that is annoying enough. (If you don't think so now, just wait. You soon will understand.) But what is really, really bone chilling is that it is not just family and friends who will want to touch the baby belly. The ladies in the supermarket will simply need to put their hands on the belly. Every kid that you encounter when you are shopping is going to touch your belly, or at least ask if they can. Heck, even the mailman might see the belly and feel the desire to touch it. People come out of nowhere to touch a pregnant belly and they could care less to whom that belly is attached. It is just something about that pregnancy belly that people find irresistible. You can politely ask people not to do it, but if you are like most moms you will just suck it up and go with it. It's kind of nice to be fussed about after all.

People Love to Talk

These is really no way to know what will come out of the mouths of some people upon learning that you are pregnant, so do not let anything that you hear surprise you. Sometimes, it is information that is very much unwanted, but it is all given to you with the best of intentions, in most cases. Be prepared for people to tell you things that you should be doing differently, giving you stories of how they did things and so much more. It is just a part of being pregnant, and yet another one of those things that everyone goes through while she is with child. Being prepared to hear some pretty off-the-wall statements can make dealing with them easier.

You will also want to prepare to be called "Mom" or "Mommy" by everyone. Kids love to do this, but adults are also in on it, too. This one isn't so bad, but it might come as a shock to hear it from some people, if you are not at least prepared to hear it

It is kind of nice to be called a mom, but the real treat comes when your baby says it the first time!

Stretch Marks

You have probably been waiting to see those two words this whole guide, wondering why you have yet to see any mention. But do not worry. We haven't forgotten them. We still look at them every single day so there is always that constant reminder there, even if we wanted to forget. People will tell you a lot about stretch marks. Every person has a different tale to tell: how to prevent them or how lucky she was not to get them. It is true that not all pregnant women get stretch marks, but for most women it is impossible to prevent them. If you are one of the lucky people for whom this is not an issue, you can thank your lucky stars for that. Stretch marks occur on the stomach, the arms and the legs, and oftentimes on the beasts, too. They occur due to the increase in the size, which stretches the skin, in such a short period of time. Stretch marks are often nice to see and they have a blue, red or purplish color. African American and Hispanic woman, as well as those of other dark skinned tones, are more likely to develop stretch marks and they are usually darker and deeper on these skin tones. There is not a lot that you can do about stretch marks. Watching what you eat so you do not gain a ton of extra weight is one step. Investing in a good cocoa butter lotion and using it on a regular basis can also help.

What's That Smell?

Have you ever wondered what it is like to be a drug-sniffing dog that has such a heightened sense of smell it can detect the faintest whiff of something? Well, we haven't either, but that is pretty much what it is like to be pregnant. You can smell everything and it is really intense. Many times you will find yourself asking, "What's that smell?" only to have other people tell you that they smell nothing. That is impossible, you think, because you can smell it so well. Your dog-like sense of smell is likely to develop at the very beginning of your pregnancy and continue until you have the baby. Sometimes it is a good thing and sometimes it is not, because you smell it all -- good and bad! Be prepared to have a Wonder Woman sense of smell.

The Movements Are Incredible

The first time that you feel your baby kick is an incredible feeling. It is incredible to feel all of his tiny little flutters and movements. Some people feel them earlier than others, but if you are paying close attention, you will be able to feel them quickly. Be sure that you have your journal ready to write all of these special feelings down.

Document Everything

This is probably not something that you will have any trouble doing. Most pregnant women love to take photos of their baby belly and their pregnancy, but many fail to keep a journal to document those special occasions. Do not assume that you are going to remember everything because you are not. Believe us, Mommy, you have yet to learn. There are tons of themed pregnancy journals and keepsake baby books that let you jot down those special memories and you very well should take advantage and use them. Remembering how you felt that first time you heard the sounds of that tiny heartbeat, how in love you were the moment that you found out, the first ultrasound and glimpse of your baby. These are all things that you want to document, but don't forget those other little and unexpected things. They are just as memorable and certainly a blast to look back upon later in life. Snap pictures until your snapping finger hurts, and keep everything special that happens to you documented in that special journal. You will be glad that you did this later in life.

"I Want It and I Want It NOW"

Ordinarily in life, we see something that we want and we get it when we can. Yes, some things we want more than we want other things, but nonetheless we understand and do what we can to work on getting those items. But when you are pregnant, you will have cravings that are so intense that not getting what you want at that very moment is enough to send you into a tear-filled frenzy for hours on end. The cravings of pregnant women are immense, and sometimes they are also very odd. The body craves what it is lacking in most cases, so if you are eating healthy you are less likely to have those cravings. For most women, though, there will be something that you simply cannot live without and would drive 500 miles to get it. Expect this.

Hemorrhoids

Yep, the real pain in the butt. Hemorrhoids are for old people who aren't eating their Raisin Bran. That notion is incorrect. Anyone can get a hemorrhoid at any age, and when you are pregnant the odds of its happening are even greater. It doesn't matter if you're 20 or 40; pregnancy doubles the risk of hemorrhoids. Again, it is all about the added pressure on the body, the rectal area and the weight of the uterus. Hemorrhoids really hurt, and that pain intensifies while you are pregnant. You may or may not get a hemorrhoid, but it is important to know it is possible. If you have a hemorrhoid, it is difficult to go to the bathroom and it also makes it difficult to sit, lie down or do much of anything else. There are many over-the-counter treatments for hemorrhoids, should you be one of the unlucky ones who develop them. You can also talk to your doctor about treatment options, if you are getting them on a frequent basis, if the over-the-counter products are not working or if you are simply concerned with baby's health and want the expert advice first. You can also help lower the odds of getting a hemorrhoid by eating a well-balanced diet. It isn't just the Raisin Bran that can help with a hemorrhoid; many fruits and vegetables are high in fiber content.

Four Weeks & a Wake-Up

The last month of pregnancy is definitely the hardest. While the last trimester itself is uneasy, it is those last four weeks that seem to make even the calmest, gentlest of people feel as if are going to lose their minds. Prepare to be uneasy all of the time and probably really grumpy and biting the heads off of everyone who so much as speaks to you. Emotions and mood swings are also going to be really high. Remember, all of those hormones are going crazy inside of your body! Everything is going to make you cry, and there may be people who are looking at you with a lot of wonder in their eyes. Ignore them. If they are mothers, they will understand. The last four weeks also seem like an eternity, so expect that to be something that you experience as well. Soon you will be free, but in the meantime prepare yourself and everyone around you for this last month. Once they have been warned, all is fair in pregnancy.

First Time Mom
Chapter 8: Your Diet And Nutrition

Diet and nutrition is key to healthy pregnancy, and often the best solution to your prenatal care. Diet is the sum of the food you eat to meet your nutritional requirements. Nutrition is how you consume and use food to nourish your body. These two go hand in hand. You need to eat a well-balanced diet to receive good nutrition your body needs for healthy pregnancy.

Healthy Diet to Meet Nutritional Needs

Nutritional needs and requirements vary depending on a number of factors such as age, gender, weight, health condition, and whether one is pregnant or not. Being pregnant, you have specific nutritional needs and requirements you should satisfy to keep your body and the life inside your body healthy. The best way to give your body good nutrition is to eat a well-balanced diet.

Earlier, you already have an idea of how much weight you should add to help you and your baby grow safe and healthy the entire span of your pregnancy. This time, you will know why eating a healthy diet is necessary to your nutrition and how it can satisfy your nutritional requirements to make sure of your safe and healthy childbirth.

Your Nutritional Needs and Requirements

While nutritional needs and requirements may vary from one pregnant woman to another, here are some standards:

You need roughly 300 added calories day-to-day. This amount can go either up or down depending on your prenatal weight together with your activity level. If you happen to carry twins in your womb, the standard increases from 300 to 500 more calories daily.

While you measure the standard in terms of quantity or the number of calories, it is crucial that you also pay attention to the quality of your caloric intake, or the kind of food that you consume. You should get your calories from healthy or nutritious food.

- Increased amount of Vitamin D. You have to know that your baby is entirely dependent on your body to meet his/her need for Vitamin D. If you are not meeting your own need for this type of vitamin, you cannot expect your baby to meet his or her own, too. Lack of this vitamin has negative effects to the physical and intellectual development of your child.
- Extra Vitamin C of about ten (10) mg daily. Your blood carries Vitamin C to different parts in your body to your baby. During this travel, you may lose a certain amount. The standard recommended allowance is 80 to 85 mg. The limit is 1800 for 18 years and below, and 2000 for 19 years and above.
- What Vitamin C does is to protect your body and your baby from infection, to strengthen bones, to repair tissues, to stimulate mental development, and to help your body absorb an essential nutrient for pregnancy that is iron.
- Folic acid or folate to prevent your unborn to contract neural defects and cleft palate. It is best to supply your body with the right amount of folate before your pregnancy and or within the first two (2) months of your term. 200 to 400 mg each day during your trimester lowers the risks for neural tube defects (birth defects that affect the mental development and spinal cord of your baby).
- Riboflavin or Vitamin B2 of 0.3 mg more each day protects your baby from heart defects, and increase in Vitamin B12 of

0.2 mg daily will help your body cope with fetus development.

The recommended amount for other nutrients stays the same for both pregnant and non-pregnant women. It is important that you meet at least the minimum standard or requirement in your nutrition. This is to give your baby the healthy environment it needs for normal growth and development until he/she is born. Depriving your body of nutrients can result to birth defects and health problems, and can even endanger both lives, yours and your baby's.

What Makes a Healthy Prenatal Diet

Your diet is the primary source to satisfy your prenatal nutrition. You have to watch your diet more carefully for the growth and development of the life you carry in your womb. Eating a healthy and well-balanced diet is a must, especially for first time moms like you.

A well-balanced prenatal diet consists of the following:

- Carbohydrates, particularly the complex type, for energy you and your baby need. The Food and Drug Administration (FDA) suggests that you should get 55% of your daily calorie need from carbohydrates.
- Choose complex carbohydrates. The body uses them longer reducing fat build-up. What you get is more energy and healthier weight gain from its consumption. They are also a good source of fiber that can help you control unnecessary food cravings.
- Protein is extremely important, as it is the nutrient that builds the foundation of good health. You should give your body about 60-70 grams of protein daily while pregnant or 15-25 gram increase from the usual daily nutrient recommendation.

The building block of cell development, protein and its amino acids are the primary nutrients responsible for fetus growth and development. Lack of it will result to several health issues and birth defects, most of which are life-endangering.

- Dietary fiber dramatically reduces the risks for health complications during your pregnancy. This is because fiber cleanses your body to flush out toxic substances. These substances are major contributors of health issues such as gestational diabetes.
- Fiber comes in two types, soluble and insoluble. Both are necessary, as each has its own specific benefits. Soluble fiber helps prevent gestational diabetes while insoluble fiber aids the digestive system and prevents constipation. Fiber will enable you to sustain healthy weight the entire course of your pregnancy.
- Vitamins and minerals are essential nutrients to keep you and your baby healthy. Remember that your baby is dependent upon you for his/her growth and development inside your womb. Essential vitamins and minerals protect the good health of your body and stimulate the best growth and development of your baby.

Certain types of food are rich in vitamins and minerals you need, such as fruits and vegetables. Natural food types are definitely better than processed food as sources of nutrients. In fact, health experts recommend natural over processed or instant food especially during pregnancy so your body receives the most nutrients you can get naturally from food.

- Water is the best way to hydrate your body, and hydration is a critical element during pregnancy. You lose more water in your body with frequent urination and perspiration while conceiving your child. You therefore need to increase your intake of water to replace what you have lost.

When your body becomes dehydrated due to lack of water, you may suffer from infection affecting the life inside you. Dehydration can also induce you to labor prematurely. To prevent unnecessary risks and complications, hydrate your body by drinking plenty of water. When it comes to drinking water, there can never be too much.

Food to Eat While Pregnant

During your pregnancy, certain food types can bring you the most benefits to improve your health and to make sure of the right nourishment for your baby. It is always best to choose food that has the most nutrients that can keep your healthy weight. Remember you need to add just the right amount of weight while you are pregnant.

The top ten foods when it comes to combined nutrients they have are the following (in no particular order):

- Asparagus is rich in fiber, folic acid, and iron, three of the most important nutrients your body should receive during pregnancy.
- Soy has vegetable protein, choline, fiber, folic acid, iron, potassium, and zinc.
- Legumes and beans are rich sources of vegetable protein, fiber, folate, iron, potassium, and zinc.
- Quinoa is a healthy seed that has lots of protein, folate, iron, and potassium.
- Milk has loads of essential vitamins and minerals like Vitamin D, B2, B12, calcium, and protein.
- Eggs are good sources of protein, choline, Vitamin B12, and selenium.

- Berries will supply your body with Vitamin C, fiber, folic acid, and they are also wealthy sources of antioxidants to protect your body from free radicals.
- Avocados are good sources of essential fats, choline, fiber, iron, potassium, and zinc.
- Salmon contains Omega 3 fatty acids, protein, Vitamin B12, and DHA or Docosahexaenoic acid, an essential fatty acid crucial to brain development.
- Yogurt has probiotic as well as Vitamin B12, calcium, and potassium.

The top ten food rich in folate or folic acid are the following (in no particular order and other than those mentioned above):

- Green leafy vegetables such as spinach. You can eat them as side dish or one of the main courses to for a well-balanced diet.
- Citrus fruits such as oranges. You can eat the fresh fruit for snack, extract the juice for refreshing beverage, or use it as an ingredient in preparing your healthy meal.
- Broccoli gives you about 24% of folate you need. It is also a savory way to detoxify your body naturally and safely during pregnancy.
- Lentils have high-density folic acid. Eating half a cup of lentils can satisfy 50% of your folate need.
- Sunflower seeds are versatile way to add folate to your diet. You can eat a handful as is as your snack, sprinkle it on your vegetable or fruit salad, and use it as an ingredient for baking. To get the most benefit, choose the unsalted variant.
- Tomatoes are also rich in folate. You can eat it raw, drink its juice, or use it as main ingredient such as with tomato soup.
- Okra is slimy but it is one vegetable loaded with folate. You can get about 37mcg of folic acid from a cup of cooked (preferably boiled or streamed) okra.

- Celery can give you 34 mcg of folate per cup. It is preferable to eat this vegetable raw or as ingredient to your fresh vegetable salad.
- Carrots are a delicious source of folic acid. It is also one of the most versatile sources to meet your daily nutrient need.

Whole grains and fortified cereals are folate boosters. Pair them with other folate sources such as broccoli, sunflower seeds, tomato juice, and others, you will experience dramatic increase in folate to satisfy your daily nutritional need.

The top ten food rich in iron (in no particular order) are the following:

Spinach is a super food that does not only contain loads of iron but other pregnancy nutrients as well. You can get about 3.2 mg of iron eating just half a cup of this super food.

Beef is a good source of iron, but choose lean beef meat for healthier way to get your nutrient. Each serving of beef meat can give you up to 3 mg of iron.

Each potato can give you 2.7 mg of iron. It is also a good source of your dietary fiber.

White beans have the highest concentration of iron among beans. It can easily give you 3.9 mg of iron per half cup.

Fortified cereals can start your day supplying your body anywhere between 2 mg to 21 mg of iron per bowl. What is best about these cereals is they are also rich in calcium and folic acid.

Prunes can satisfy both your iron and fiber needs. You can choose to eat the dried fruit or drink the juice; they both give you the same iron content.

Seaweed is rich in iron and a safe way to get Omega 3 fatty acids. It is also a good alternative to fish oils necessary for mental development of your baby.

Pumpkin seeds can really pump up your iron supply. You can eat its roasted seeds as snack, or include it as a recipe ingredient for texture and taste.

Clam chowder can give you about 23 mg of iron per bowl. Use tomato as soup base and you double the benefits, since the Vitamin C in tomato will allow your body to absorb the iron better. Tomato is also a good source of folic acid.

Liver pâté is very rich in iron. Chicken liver has high concentration of iron followed by beef liver. If you want to get the highest iron content, choose goose liver for your pâté recipe. Prepare just enough for immediate consumption as refrigerating it can expose the pâté to bacteria.

Food You Should Refrain from Eating

If certain food types help you satisfy your nutritional needs, there are those you should avoid while you are pregnant. The American Pregnancy Association lists the food as follows:

Uncooked seafood like oysters and raw meat from pork, beef, and poultry. Eating them puts you and your baby at risk for disease-causing bacteria such as salmonella. It can also cause food poisoning, which of course endangers your lives.

Fish with concentrated levels of mercury such as swordfish, shark, king mackerel among others. You can eat canned tuna but be very conservative in eating it. As much as possible avoid eating sushi or raw fish meat. To satisfy your Omega 3 fatty acid needs, you can choose to take natural dietary supplements such as fish oil. Consult your physician before taking any supplements.

Uncooked eggs to avoid the risk of salmonella. Be sure to check the ingredients as some readily available food such as mayonnaise, dressings, ice creams, or certain types of sauces and dips may use raw eggs. This is especially true for homemade recipes.

Soft types of cheese unless they only have pasteurized milk as ingredient can put you at risk for miscarriage. Similarly refrain from drinking unpasteurized milk as like soft cheese, it has Listeria, bacteria that can travel in your body to your baby and cause blood poisoning.

Caffeinated beverages can trigger miscarriages, low birth weight of your baby, and or premature childbirth. Caffeine works as a diuretic to rid of body fluids. It can result to dehydration and nutrient loss. Beverages that contain caffeine are coffee, tea, or sodas. Drink plenty of water instead. To add flavor and taste to water, you can choose to drink milk, fresh fruit or vegetable juices. You should remember though that they are not substitutes for your water necessity.

Avoid alcohol at all costs. Even the smallest amount of alcohol can already interfere with how the life inside your womb develops. It can cause serious harmful effects to your baby. Before, during, and after your pregnancy especially if you are to breastfeed your baby, you should refrain from drinking alcoholic beverages.

Unwashed fruits and vegetables. Especially with vegetables, they may contain traces of pesticides or toxic substances from the soil. It is also best to choose organic vegetables or homegrown fruits, as they are safer and has higher concentration of nutrients.

First Time Mom

Natural Dietary Supplements

You may not meet your nutritional needs from your healthy diet alone. This is especially true for women who are not used to eating nutritious food before getting pregnant. To increase guarantee of giving the body essential nutrients, it is crucial to take dietary supplements.

However, you must exercise extreme caution and care in choosing your supplements. It is best to pick all natural food supplements that come from reliable and trustworthy manufacturers. You should also see to it to consult your physician before you take any supplements regardless of how safe they are.

Food Supplements Safe for Pregnancy

Several natural dietary supplements are available in the market. While they all claim to deliver safe results even for pregnancy, not all can bring health benefits. A few of these supplements, however, are necessary and important, some can do more harm than good, and the rests have no use at all.

Four (4) natural food supplements that are safe to take during pregnancy are the following:

Prenatal multivitamins - this is typically what physicians prescribed or recommend to their pregnant patients. It supplies the body with a combination of essential vitamins and minerals necessary for pregnancy such as iron, Vitamin B complex and D, calcium, and there are brands that have a substantial amount of folic acid as well.

Folic acid or folate - when you prenatal multivitamin does not include folate or folic acid, you can get it separately. Folic acid prevents birth defects. To maximize benefits from this nutrient, you should consume the food supplements before your pregnancy and or during the first trimester, and from then on increase the dosage up to the recommended limit.

Fiber dietary supplements are typically safe for use by pregnant women. These natural supplements help regulate hormones in the body that fluctuate during pregnancy. Fiber improves food digestion and prevents constipation. It is important that you drink a lot of water while taking dietary fiber supplements.

Fish oil food supplements are good sources of Omega 3 fatty acids. This is particularly useful to avoid harmful mercury in most fish meats. The supplements supply the body with essential fatty acids without the risks of exposure to mercury. Stay away from cod liver oil, though, as the amount of Vitamin A it has can bring adverse effects to your baby.

In choosing your food supplements, exercise extra care and caution. This is the time when being meticulous has the most benefit. See to it that you read the label and get all pertinent information about the product. Limit your choice only to those products that come from trusted brands and manufacturers. Ingredients must be all natural or organic and only the finest.

Most importantly, make sure that you consult with your physician before taking any of these food supplements. You can get recommendations from your physician and or discuss your options in taking dietary supplements to boost the meeting of or satisfaction of your nutritional needs. While food is the primary source of nutrients, supplements can fill in the gap to increase assurance that you are meeting your recommended daily intake of nutrients for your pregnancy.

What You Can Benefit from Food Supplements

First Time Mom

The right choice of dietary supplements can bring several benefits to your pregnancy. They are the secondary sources of nutrients. Your healthy diet may not meet your specific nutritional needs. This is where supplements come in handy as they fill in the gap.

You have to keep in mind that the life inside your womb is completely dependent on your body for nourishment. When you eat, you do not just think about your own needs but also the nutritional needs of the baby you are carrying. Any nutritional deficiency on your body can take its toil on your baby.

It is also quite tedious to source all your nutrients from food. You will have to really plan hard and well and eat a lot to meet your needs. The least you would want is unnecessary stress and pressure as they are unhealthy for your baby. Dietary supplements help your body receive nutrients it needs without added calories from food.

Natural food supplements ease the burden of satisfying your nutritional needs. It does not mean, however, that you will depend your needs heavily on these supplements since they bring convenient results. As much as you can, you must source your essential nutrients from your healthy diet, as this is the best method you and your baby can benefit from your nutrition. Supplements should come in only as a gap filler. Some nutrients are difficult to source from food owing to your delicate condition.

Improve your dietary habits and start paying attention to the quality your food intake. Choose those that are highly nutritious, those that are rich in nutrients specific to healthy pregnancy but low in calories. Strive hard to meet your daily nutritional needs from food and fill in the gap by taking the right supplements. This is the best way to nourish your body so you and your baby get the most benefits.

Chapter 9: Your Diet And Common Health Issues

Do you know that your diet plays a major role in treating and resolving common health issues during pregnancy? Often, it is the best and only solution you need to get well from health problems and ailments during your maternity period.

Natural Remedies for Morning Sickness

Morning sickness, or joint bouts of nausea and vomiting, is a popular symptom of pregnancy. Most pregnant women experience this symptom usually during the first three months. For some women, morning sickness can last the entire trimester and occurs not only in the mornings but also throughout the day.

To deal with this symptom effectively, you have to understand what triggers it. The main culprit for morning sickness is the fluctuation of your hormones, specifically the rise of your beta HCG or what you call as your pregnancy hormone.

Typically, nausea and vomiting is self-limiting. For pregnant women, this symptom goes away after the first trimester. Certain studies show that morning sickness is a mechanism of the body to protect you and your baby from the harmful effects of toxic substances.

With morning sickness comes your aversion for certain food. Amazingly, food items that you learn to hate are the types that have the most harmful chemicals. To relieve yourself of the symptom, a good natural remedy is to eat dry crackers or cereals. They are also rich in fiber and iron, two of the nutrients pregnant women need.

It also helps to limit your food intake to smaller portions but increase its frequency. You have to make sure that you are meeting your recommended nutrition with the amount and quality of food you eat. To prevent nausea and vomiting, drink your water at least half an hour before meals. You can also choose to drink it half an hour after meals. Drink plenty of water in between meals to hydrate your body.

It is best to stay away from spices and oily food. Choose to eat food that has less odor, as the smell can trigger you to feel nauseous and vomit. Ask your spouse or anyone in the family to take over the cooking chores, at least during the first trimester of your pregnancy. Give your body enough sleep.

Skin-Friendly Diet

Skin disorders and irritations are common to pregnant women, but these are the types that normally disappear after childbirth. If you want to keep your skin healthy, here is what food to eat and what food to avoid.

What Food to Eat

Here are at least five (5) food you should that serves as good nourishment for your skin. They contain nutrients to protect your skin from hormonal fluctuations to prevent or relieve skin irritations and disorders.

Avocado is rich in Vitamin E and antioxidants to protect your skin cells against damages from free radicals. This fruit has glutathione to help lighten the skin from hyper-pigmentation and keep it younger-looking.

Sweet potatoes are a power-packed source of nutrients containing Vitamins A, C, and E beneficial to the skin. You will benefit from the beta-carotene content of this food to prevent aging of the skin, specifically to delay wrinkles from showing.

Tomatoes have wealth of Vitamin C that builds collagen (protein necessary for tissue connection and support). It is also a good source of Lycopene, a substance that protects the skin from sun damage.

Walnuts keep the skin smooth and supple because of its alpha linolenic acid content. This nut is also a good source of beta-carotene and Vitamin E, and a delicious way to enjoy the healing properties of zinc.

Olive oil protects outer skin and prevents injury. It has the healthy fats the body needs and is one of the richest sources of Vitamin E, beta-carotene, and polyphenols that protect the skin from free radicals.

What Food to Avoid

If certain food brings loads of skin benefits, there are also those that are unfriendly and can worsen your skin problems. You should refrain from eating these food types.

Sweets and other food that has excess sugar are not only villains to your weight, but they can also worsen your pre-existing skin condition such as acne or fungal infection. What is more, sweets can speed up the aging of your skin to make you look older than your age.

Alcohol is a diuretic that can dehydrate your body and show on your skin. It is one food that is a completely no-no for pregnant women. It can heighten your skin problems and trigger other health issues putting you and your baby at higher health risks.

Processed and instant food contains chemical ingredients that can further disturb your already fluctuating hormones. Prevent toxic substances to enter your body and wreak havoc by avoiding this food type.

Gestational Diabetes Diet

Gestational diabetes is a health condition specific to pregnant women and easily controllable with the right diet. It is a common ailment during pregnancy where blood sugar level rises. If you fail to manage the condition, it can have serious effects on your baby.

One of the best natural ways to manage the condition is to watch your diet. Among the food groups that have dramatic influence on gestation diabetes is carbohydrates. But you cannot abstain from eating carbohydrates without disrupting your nutritional balance.

What you can do is to shift from eating food with simple carbohydrates to those that have complex carbohydrates and strictly follow a well-balanced diet. The difference between the two types of carbohydrates is their sugar content.

Simple carbohydrates have only one or two molecules of sugar that make it the fastest to digest and absorb. Unfortunately, it is also the type that has little nutritional value except rich calories. Examples of food containing simple carbohydrates are sugar, syrups, jams, jellies, soft drinks, and candies.

In contrast, complex carbohydrates have more sugar molecules that enable the body to use it longer. Since it is slow to digest, it does not mix with the blood easily. It is the type of carbohydrates that can keep your glucose or blood sugar stable. They also contain fiber that can rid your body of toxic substances and wastes efficiently. Examples are whole grains, green vegetables, beans and peas, potatoes and sweet potatoes, pumpkin, and corn.

Since your body needs energy from carbohydrates, it is best to source your energy from eating food that has complex carbohydrates. Make sure to eat just the right amount necessary to keep your diet well balanced. It also helps to supplement your diet with essential vitamins and minerals to meet your nutritional needs. Choose natural over processed food.

Strictly follow the recommended daily dietary allowance for pregnant women. Your primary source of nutrients should come from your healthy diet. Use supplements to fill nutritional gaps. Monitor your blood sugar level all throughout your pregnancy, and consult your physician regularly.

When you satisfy the nutritional needs of your body, you are activating and strengthening its own natural mechanism to protect and prevent any health issues, problems, and or diseases. Pregnancy is a delicate condition. It is wise to use natural remedies as they work with your body and not against it. However, you should always consult your physician for any remedy you wish to apply regardless if how safe it is. Getting the best of both worlds will definitely increase guarantee of safe pregnancy especially that this is your first time.

First Time Mom
Chapter 10: Labor And Delivery

Labor and delivery carries its own set of signs and symptoms, and things you should look out for. Unlike the three trimesters of your pregnancy, these symptoms are not going to last you very long, maybe a few hours to a few days at most. Some women may experience early labor symptoms for up to a week before labor starts, but these will generally be low in intensity until they get closer to active labor.

In this chapter, we are going to explore the signs and symptoms that labor is on the way. You will also learn about some of the basic things that you should expect in the delivery room, and how you can prepare yourself for the experience.

SIGNS OF LABOR

The following symptoms are signs that labor is preparing to start. These symptoms are generally felt at some point between 37-40 weeks, if you carry your pregnancy all the way to term. However, you may experience these symptoms earlier than that if you are going into preterm labor. If you start experiencing any of these symptoms, especially before 37 weeks, you should consult your doctor. They will tell you what to do, and when you should come in!

YOUR BABY "DROPS" INTO POSITION

Before labor starts, your baby will "drop" into position. You can tell this has happened when your baby bump is sitting lower down, and is more directed towards your pelvis. This is because the baby has officially prepared to enter the birth canal, so they are getting lined up and ready to make an appearance!

YOUR CERVIX DILATES

Probably the most well-known symptom of labor starting is the cervix dilating. Of course, you probably can't tell this is happening, but your doctor will be able to tell you. In the days leading up to your labor, your cervix will begin to slowly dilate. Most women sit around 1-2cm for about a week or two before labor actually begins. Once labor starts, they will continue opening until they reach 10cm, which is when active labor starts.

INCREASED CRAMPING AND LOWER BACK PAIN

You may notice more pain in your lower back and more cramping in your abdomen. This occurs as a result of your muscles preparing to put in all of the work to release your baby. This can also happen because the new position of your baby results in there being new pressures on your lower back and pelvic area. As well, your pelvis will be opening up the last little amount to let your baby come out, so your bones are quite literally stretching open.

LOOSER JOINTS

The increased progesterone in your system are still responsible for your joints being loose, though you may notice this even more towards labor. You may experience popping or cracking in your joints a lot more, particularly when you move out of a position you've been sitting in for the same amount of time for a while.

DIARRHEA

Many women experience diarrhea leading up to labor. This can be a displeasing opposite of the constipation that many women experience in the weeks beforehand. If you experience this, it's just because your muscles are loosening which means so are your bowel movements. Make sure you drink plenty of water, and prepare for labor to start!

YOUR WEIGHT GAIN SLOWS DOWN, OR YOU LOSE SOME WEIGHT

Once your baby is fully "cooked" they will pretty much stop putting on weight, because they are getting ready to come out! So, if you notice you've stopped putting on pounds, or even if you lose a couple, this is why!

YOU FEEL MORE FATIGUED THAN NORMAL

Because of your super-sized belly and all of your hormones, and the frequent need to urinate, it can be hard to get a full nights' rest. Because of this, you may find that you are consistently tired. The best thing you can do is sleep on the side closest to the washroom, and keep several pillows on hand to make those few hours of shut eye as restful as possible. As well, rest as much during the day as you can.

YOU START NESTING

This is a common symptom of labor that you see often in the media on television shows and in movies. Nesting is a symptom many pregnant women experience towards the end of pregnancy as a means to prepare their home for the baby. If you find you suddenly have a burst of energy and all you want to do is clean and get everything ready for baby to come, it could be because baby is coming very soon!

YOUR VAGINAL DISCHARGE CHANGES

Changes in vaginal discharge can include increased or thickened discharge, and a change in color. This is completely normal.

YOUR CONTRACTIONS BECOME STRONGER AND MORE REGULAR

As your Braxton Hicks contractions change to actual contractions, you may notice they become a lot stronger and more regular in frequency. This is your body preparing to contract the baby out, and unless they are happening minutes apart for a long period of time, it is completely normal.

BLOODY SHOW/MUCUS PLUG

As well as your vaginal discharge changing, you may experience your bloody show at some point. This happens as your mucus plug starts to fall out. You may notice a snot-like consistency that is streaked with blood. This is your mucus plug, and you don't need to worry about this, unless it's coming out before 37 weeks! Either way, you should tell this to your doctor just so they can be prepared for your impending labor!

YOUR WATER BREAKS

The water breaking is one of the most famously known labor symptoms, but also happens to be one of the ones that happen the least! Only about 15% of women experience this symptom, and it's usually the last sign that labor is about to start. Make sure you let your doctor know as soon as your water breaks, especially if it breaks early.

WHAT YOU SHOULD EXPECT IN THE DELIVERY ROOM

There are a lot of things to expect in the delivery room, and it varies based on how your pregnancy and labor have gone. If you are carrying a high-risk pregnancy, if you have a scheduled caesarean section, or if something goes wrong and your labor becomes an emergency caesarean section, you are going to have a totally different experience in the delivery room. In this chapter, we are going to only discuss what to expect in a healthy pregnancy where delivery occurs in a hospital room.

The delivery room is a scary and exciting place, and you may become overwhelmed with emotion while you are there. You are going to be going through a lot physically, and mentally. You are preparing to meet the life you've been creating for the past nine months, and that is a lot to take in! You are likely going to get hooked up to a no-stress-test machine that will make sure your fetal movements are strong and healthy, and to measure your contractions. You are also going to get your cervix checked on a fairly regular basis, to see how far you are progressing.

A good portion of your stay is going to be spent relaxing as much as possible so that you have the energy to get through the contractions. You may wish to spend some time in the shower or on a birthing ball, to help take some of the pressure and pain off of your abdomen. If it gets really hard, you may opt for pain medicines, such as laughing gas, or an epidural. If you were GBS positive, you will also be hooked up to an IV to get antibiotics every four hours.

Once labor begins, your doctor and a few nurses will come into the room. They will help coach you through pushing, and make sure your baby comes out safely. Your doctor may use forceps or a vacuum extractor to help take out your baby, if he or she needs a little assistance on the way out. Once your baby is out, your doctor will clamp the umbilical cord and let your partner cut the cord, if you have a partner involved. Then, you will be given a chance to have skin-to-skin contact with your baby, and nurse him or her. Sometime after your baby has been born, you will also have to push out your placenta, which is not a painful experience for most women, and takes minimal effort. The placenta is a tissue, so it will not stretch out your vagina as it exits your body, meaning you will likely not find it to be as painful, or painful at all.

Shortly after your baby is born, the nurses will take him or her for a few minutes to weigh your baby, and take some important measurements. You will then be able to shower off, and move into a more permanent room where you will remain for the rest of your hospital stay. About twenty-four hours after your baby is born, they will have their vitals taken to ensure that your baby is not suffering from jaundice or anything else. These are called heel-poke tests and they only take a few minutes for to do. Throughout the time you are there, your nurses will come in to check on you and your baby to ensure that you are both getting along well, and provide you with any support or assistance you may need along the way.

AN INSIGHT TO POSTPARTUM LIFE

The initial postpartum period is the hardest. You will be in "fourth trimester" until about six weeks after your baby is born. At this point, you are going to experience your postpartum bleeding, and many hormonal changes. Your body will be getting back into a balance from all of the pregnancy hormones, which can lead to many emotional and physical changes.

During these weeks, your baby is still going to have part of the umbilical cord - complete with the clamp - attached to their body. This will naturally fall off within' a few days once it dries up. Your baby may spit up a lot, which is completely normal as they are getting used to being able to digest food. Their poop is also weird, as it will be a blackish green color, or it could be yellow or brown. The color of newborn poop varies, and can also vary in texture. As long as it is not pale, you should be okay.

Getting to sleep through the night will be hard with your newborn, as they will want to eat frequently. Ideally, you should sleep during the day when your baby sleeps, at least for the first little while, as this will help you replenish the sleep you are losing through waking up all hours of the night. Having a strong support system in place is also helpful.

Chapter 11: What to Expect - Labor Induction

Many women hear the topic of induction and they do not know exactly how to respond. The thought that your body does not want to go into labor on its own, or that your baby would be safer if they were delivered under a medical induction can be terrifying. However, if you take the time to understand the process, it will not be nearly as scary as it sounds.

What is Medical Labor Induction?

There are many medical reasons to have your labor induced. Your body naturally creates the hormones necessary to start your labor. However, some women do not create enough of the hormone to really get labor going strong enough to bring your baby into this world. Sometimes, your body just needs a little boost.

When your doctor has decided that it is time to induce your labor, he will give you an IV medication called pitocin. This will help start contractions and help to thin out your cervix.

Who Should Be Considered for Induction?

There are many reasons that your doctor may consider you for induction. These reasons are:

- gestational diabetes
- pre-eclampsia
- going past your due date (41 weeks pregnant)
- if the health of you and your baby are at risk by continuing the pregnancy
- … and other medical conditions that affect you and baby

What about inducing for non-medical reasons?

First Time Mom

Are you just tired of being pregnant? Or does your doctor have something planned during the time of your due date? Does this have you thinking about inducing early? Did you know that almost 25 percent of the inductions are not medically necessary or are elective according to the Center for Disease Control Moms and experts are hot on the topic of induced labor during non-medical reasons.

Inducing before 39 weeks have not been recommended by the American College of Obstetricians and Gynecologists. If you induce earlier than 39 weeks there is a risk of bringing a child into the world that is not fully developed. "Induction can carry risks that should only be used for medical reasons," says Sabine Droste, MD. She is a professor at the University of Wisconsin-Madison of obstetrics and gynecology.

There are certain situations where if the doctor thinks that they are close to deliver but live too far away or won't make the drive to the hospital the doctor may make a call to induce. This would keep a birth from happening on the road, or anywhere outside of the hospital.

What are the risks of non-medical induction?

There are times when family come to see the birth of your child or we are so busy that we would like to have the delivery at a certain time. This can cause for a treat amount of temptation to induce your pregnancy because of this. Other times people think and say that you are too big and you will have to have a C-section in order to have your child. This can scare mothers to try and induce labor before truly knowing if the baby really is too big or not.

You should really think about this and be cautious because you could complicate things. Just because you induce early does not mean you will not need to have a C-section. The chances of having a C-section are about as equal of a chance as the baby actually being too big to need a C-section. You should wait to make this decision after discussing with your doctor the options you have taken and thought about.

How is labor induced?

When there is a patient that has a cervix that is insufficiently dilated, the cervix needs to be softened. We do this by using prostaglandin which is a hormone. After the cervix is softened another hormone called oxytocin is administered to help trigger labor. Pitocin is usually intravenously administered. Inducing labor is much easier when there are already signs of labor early on. This is because the body is ready to go.

There are other ways of inducing labor, such as breaking the amniotic sac releasing the amniotic fluid. This is done by puncturing the amniotic sac with a sterile plastic like hook. When the amniotic fluid is released it contains prostaglandins. This will help to increase the frequency and strength of your contractions. If this does not induce labor than there is a larger risk that infection can spread to your baby because there are no fluids to protect the baby any more.

There is a different procedure called membrane sweeping. This involves breaking the membrane connections from the uterus. This is supposed to force the cervix to start dilating and effacing which should help to start contractions.

Although these are methods that are used, it does not mean that they will always work. It all depends on how the mothers body will react when these actions are taken. The mothers body can react differently to any of these. It could cause labor to run fast and smooth or it could make things take longer.

Do natural inducers really work?

First Time Mom

Here are popular methods that are used. You can decide for yourself if they are effective.

Walking has been used to try and help move the baby into a position that uses gravity that can help.

Stimulating your nipples can help release oxytocin and can start contractions. Although doctors give caution to this method because it can also cause contractions that will last longer and cause distress to your baby.

The Pineapple fruit has a chemical in it called bromelain. This can help to soften the tissues connected to the cervix.

Sex can be a fun way of trying to speed things along. This is because semen has cervix-softening prostaglandins in it.

Spicy foods can also help kick the body into full gear and get your innards moving. But if it does not work it could just cause you to have gas.

Chapter 12: What to Expect – Having a C-Section

There are so many women who have their birth plan in mind through their full pregnancy.

They have memorized and read about all the details. Many end up learning that the best chance for the safety of their child is for them to be delivered through C-section. This can be upsetting when this was not the plan they had in mind all this time. This change in plans can cause the feeling of fear, guild and dread causing them to tailspin. In all reality women should always keep in mind that things can and may happen to change how the delivery of their baby may go.

The C-section is no way any woman wants the birth to go but in certain situations it becomes necessary. Here we will discuss what you can expect if your doctor says the better way is to have a C-section. Sometimes the doctor may call that a C-section should be done because of certain complications that the doctor has noticed. Other times it happens during labor when the baby is not reacting well with the contractions you are having.

When a mother hears C-section mentioned it automatically causes fear to develop. We will discuss issues that are common with unplanned C-sections.

Typical Immediate Fears

C-sections are commonly talked about and how they are so awful. This can cause instant dread and questions to flood your mind. Some of these worries are would it ruin my experience of birth? Will there be an excruciating and long recovery time? Would I be left with big ugly scars?

Will this C-section be unnecessary?

The decision in performing a C-section is made by 2 physicians. They are quite common and happen in 1 out of 4 births. Some reasons that C-sections are taken into account are for multiple pregnancy, large baby, labor failure, diabetic medical conditions, fetal distress, placenta Previa or high blood pressure.

Will the Surgery Be Long and Scary?

It is normal for any major surgery to make you apprehensive. You will feel pressure and a slight tugging when they pull the baby out. It should be a painless procedure that takes around 45 minutes. The baby is usually born within 10 to 15 minutes from the start of the operation.

Most of the C-section is performed with the mother awake. To relieve pain, the mother can have a spinal block or epidural which will numb the lower portion of the body.

Epidurals are usually used in labor and it will be topped off before the surgery of a C-section. The Spinals are given when there is a scheduled cesarean. They last only about 1 or 2 hours and can be easily administered. They reserve general anesthesia in rare cases or emergencies when the spinal or epidural does not work.

The surgery starts with an incision above the bikini line into the abdomen wall. A second incision is made in the uterus wall where the delivery of the baby takes place. They then cut the umbilical cord and remove the placenta and close the incisions.

First Time Mom

When the surgery is all done Duramorph is usually administered for a long-lasting pain reliever. This helps for any discomfort after the spinal or epidural has stopped working.

Will this rob me of the experience of giving birth?

It is not a regular birth but the mother is awake and will experience her baby being delivered into this world and into her arms.

You should not blame yourself for a C-section and that the planned labor did not go as was planned. As long as the baby is healthy and delivered than the birth was a success. You should be happy that you just brought a life into this world.

Will a C-section prevent me from bonding with my baby?

When you have a C-section you are awake to witness it and most times you will have your baby handed to you right after birth. This allows for you to hold your baby and love them.

Will recovery be extremely painful and difficult?

You are held for around 4 days at the hospital where you will experience pain around the areas where the incisions were made. It will also be difficult to get out of bed and back in bed unassisted. You will be given a couple of types of drugs to help manage pain. Percocet will most likely be prescribed as a painkiller. Sometimes a morphine drip that can be self-administered will be given so that the patient can press a button when the pain gets to be too much.

There are ways that you can help to lower the pain and increase the speed of recovery. Drinking warm water has been suggested. This can help you to pass gas. This shows that you can start eating solid foods again. It is also suggested that if you have had a C-section that you get out of bed the day after surgery or as soon as possible.

First Time Mom

This helps to loosen up the muscles around the incision area and can get you back to wanting to get up and go.

Medication will help to ease the pain so that you can get out of bed and you shouldn't be afraid to use it.

When you get home keep getting up and moving but don't over work yourself and do strenuous work. You will begin to feel better in as little as a week.

Will I have a scary, ugly scar?

At first the area can be red. There will be a thin scar just above your pubic hairline. The incisions are usually 5 to 6 inches in length so that there is enough room for the shoulders and head of your baby to be delivered. Over time the color and size of your scar will face where only your husband, doctor and if you have one your bikini waxer will only see. You can also look at your scar as a happy remembrance of when you brought your child into this world.

Will all of my future babies have to be born through C-section?

Doctors for the longest time always stuck with the saying that once you had a C-section you would always have a C-section. This is no longer how it is looked at. There is now a 70% success rate of vaginal birth after cesarean and it is increasing as a safe option.

But as with any surgery there can always be more complications that can cause serious risk. You should always allow your doctor to consider and evaluate if it is an option for your next birth or not. Always make sure to consult your doctor and ask those important questions in moderation during your office visits.

Chapter 13: Preparing for Delivery

New moms have a great training tool for delivery available. Classes are a good idea for any first time mom. There are different types of classes available to any new mama that she can take advantage of. A birthing class is a great choice, you can go alone or with your partner, and you will find most hospitals offer this for first time parents. Usually this is free of charge. That is helpful because as you know you are starting to spend a lot of money on the new baby! A birthing class will walk you through delivery step by step.

Truth time. You are probably going to see a movie showing someone actually giving birth. It may make you swoon in anticipation of your big day or it may make you want to vomit. If the latter feeling overtakes you do not worry. This is normal. When it is your body and your baby it suddenly will not seem icky in any way. If you take a class at the hospital you plan to deliver at that is great because they will take you on a tour of the hospital and birthing area. Now if you find out that you will be in a room with another mom during delivery do not despair. When you are in labor you will just plain not care. All you will be focused on is working through the contractions, controlling the pain, and preparing to meet your new bundle of joy. Of course, there will be a curtain separating the two laboring mothers so you will have privacy.

Birthing classes will also teach you the importance of how to breathe. You may have seen a movie where a mom gives birth. It may seem funny when the mom is "hee hee hoo hooing" however that type of breathing is most beneficial and really does help to control the pain!

After the baby is born you will either breastfeed or bottle-feed. The choice is yours. However, you do need to be aware that breastfeeding is extremely good for your child. Especially, the first few days when the colostrum is in your breasts before your milk lets down. There may be reasons you are unsure about breastfeeding. Do you have to go back to work? You can work and breastfeed. You can pump on your lunch and breastfeed before and after work and throughout the night. You can also choose to alternate bottle and breast. Breastfeed when you are home and let the baby drink formula when you are working. That is ok! Some breast milk will still give your baby all the necessary and helpful nutrients that she needs. There will be classes after the baby is born on breastfeeding. If you are having difficulty or not sure about breastfeeding then these classes would be helpful to you. Also, most if not all hospitals have lactation consultants and they will help you. Not to mention, they will definitely understand all the feelings you are having and work you through it.

Have you thought about the birth experience yet? There are several things you need to decide. Who do you want in the room with you when you are giving birth? Yes, you may want visitors during labor and that is different than giving birth. When you are ready to push the stirrups come out and privacy disappears. The choice of who to have in the room with you when you are bringing a child into this world is a very personal decision. You may only want your partner. You may want your partner and your mom. You might not care who is in there. The hospital usually only lets two people in the room at a time though. If you originally thought that you wanted perhaps your mom or his mom in the room and you change your mind that is ok. It is hard to let someone know that you no longer want anyone in the room. This is one of the times that you will be so happy to have your nurse around. Labor and delivery nurses have no bones about telling visitors that they cannot come in the room. In fact, they will probably lie for you and say it is their decision to avoid any hurt feelings. Remember though, this is your big day! Just like a wedding you get to make the decisions. If someone's feelings get hurt that is okay, they will get over it. When you are laboring to bring your child into this world it is up to you, and only you, who is there with you.

It is a good idea to have some sort of birth plan. First up, drugs. Do you plan on getting an epidural? Do you plan on delivering natural? You should have a general idea of what you want and do not be shy about speaking up. Truth time. You may change your mind. That is ok! If you planned on going completely natural and the pain is getting too intense for you then it is okay to get the epidural. Do not feel bad about this. You are not a wimp. You are a smart woman who is doing what is best for her and her child. On the other hand, you may be doing okay and decide to hold off on the epidural and end up going natural. If you are trying to go natural and at the last minute decide you want an epidural it may be too late. There is a point where it is about to be pushing time that the doctor will no longer allow the epidural to be administered.

Another thing to decide is do you want to walk around or lie down throughout the contractions. Again, you may very well change your mind. If the contractions start to slow down walking the halls of the maternity ward can help to speed it back up. Do you want music? Do you want to use an exercise ball to roll on? No matter what you decide make sure it is about making you as comfortable as possible during the labor and delivery experience.

First Time Mom

Chapter 14: What to Expect - Bringing Baby Home

No matter how many children you have, bringing every new baby home is a unique experience. No two babies are the same, which surprises many parents. This is especially the case when they bring home a new baby and their personality is the exact opposite of their previous children. The truth is, every child is different, and many of these differences are noticeable as soon as their baby comes into this world.

Ten Important Facts About Newborns

Let's face it, you never know exactly what to expect from a newborn, especially if you are a new parent. Here are ten important facts that you should know about newborns that no one else will tell you.

1.   Your baby may look, well, strange. Baby's heads typically appear squished for a few weeks. This is because they were repeatedly squished as they passed through the birth canal. Also, newborn's faces are typically puffy and a little swollen. Some babies may have bruises on the bonier places of their face too.

2.   Your baby won't reward you for at least the first six weeks. Every parent looks forward to hearing their new baby coo and smile. Unfortunately, baby's typically do not reach these milestones until they are about six weeks old. Don't worry, it is well worth the wait.

3.   Babies must have a sponge bath until their umbilical cord falls off. This usually takes about two weeks. The good news is that babies do not really get dirty at this age, so getting a few sponge baths will not cause hygiene problems.

First Time Mom

4.   Your baby's soft spot is not as sensitive as you would think. It is just fine to brush his hair and touch his head. You may feel the soft spot pulsate when you touch it, but this is only because of the blood vessels surrounding the area.

5.   Your baby WILL let you know if she is getting enough food. Your baby should eat every two to three hours at first. However, if she is hungry more often, she will definitely let you know. Many pediatricians are slowly moving toward mothers feeding their baby's at will, rather than keeping them on a strict schedule. Over time, your baby will regulate her eating habits to a set schedule.

6.   Babies have dry skin and their isn't much you can do about it. Think about it like this. If you spent 9 months floating around in a pool and decided to get out, your skin would dry out over a few days too. While you do not technically have to do anything about it, you can apply some Johnson's pink baby lotion if it makes you feel better.

7.   You and baby are not hostages when you come home. You can come and go whenever you and baby please. The only thing you must ensure is that anyone who touches your baby must wash their hands first.

8.   Babies cry ALOT. This is how your baby communicates. These ear piercing screams will let you know that your baby is hungry, cold, has a messy diaper, or wants you to hold them. The only problem is that these early conversations can be extremely frustrating for both of you. Over time, you will learn what each wail means.

9.   Babies may sleep a lot, but they do not sleep for long stretches of time. It is important that you wake your baby up every three hours to get changed and eat. Do not wake your baby up during the night, they will wake up if they need something. By following

this schedule, your baby will learn the difference between day and night schedules.

10. The first few weeks will be the most stressed, lonely and tired days of your life. These are the difficult times that prepare you for the rest of parenting. Rest assured, it will get better faster than you think.

Leaving the Hospital

Do not overdress your newborn baby for his or her 1st trip home. If you think you will be too warm in a knitted cap during the day, think that the same will apply to your baby. It is alright to dress your baby in a baby blanket over bare legs or a T-shirt and light cotton pants when the weather is warm. During cooler or cold days, you can wrap your baby in a hat, footsie pajamas and warm blanket. But always check that the blanket is far from the face of your face to prevent him or her from being suffocated. It is also important that you choose clothes simple clothes that do not need a lot of pulling and pushing of your newborn baby's legs and arms. Before you leave the hospital, make sure that you have raised all your questions to your doctor so that you will have peace of mind when you get home.

During the Car Trip

The car seat is considered as the most essential thing you need during your baby's first trip home. All states require parents to ensure that their babies have a car seat before they leave the hospital. You can opt to buy, rent or borrow a car seat even before your due date. This will give you enough time to carefully inspect the car seat for safety. You can choose between infant-only car seats or convertible car seats. If you decide on an infant-only car seat, make sure that you replace it when your baby grows to more than 22 to 35 lbs. Many parents prefer a convertible car seat so that they will not need to buy a new one when their baby grows older.

First Time Mom

First-Time Emotions

It is natural to have mixed emotions during your baby's first trip home. This is particularly true for first-time parents. There will be both nervousness and excitement. You may also feel sore and physically drained, depending on your experiences during labor and delivery. Your mixed emotions can also be the result of hormone imbalances caused by the childbirth.

You may also start to feel anxious as you think about the needs of not only of your newborn baby but the needs of your partner and other kids, as well. Even visits from family and friends can add to your stress level. Amidst all these emotions, it is very important that you talk to and seek help from your partner and other loved ones who are willing to help.

When to Call the Doctor

Pediatricians are used to first-time moms calling them often during the first few weeks after the baby is born. First-time moms, in particular, can worry too much even for the littlest things. If ever you come to a point when you are not sure whether to call your doctor or not, here are some signs that can tell to do so immediately:

1. More than 8 diarrhea stools within eight hours.

2. Rectal temperature is 38 degrees Celsius (100.4 degrees Fahrenheit) or higher. This is particularly important for babies younger than two months.

3. Bloody stool or vomit

4. Symptoms of dehydration such as no wet diapers in six to eight hours, a depression in the soft spot on the head of the baby and sunken eyes.

5. Inability to keep fluids down or repeated forceful vomiting.

6. A soft spot that protrudes when your baby is upright and quiet.

7. Labored or rapid breathing. Immediately call 911 when you notice that your baby starts to turn bluish around the mouth or lips and has difficulty in breathing.

8. When your baby is difficult to rouse.

Always be aware of your new baby's condition. Even minor conditions can at times change rapidly for young babies.

Chapter 15: Tips for First Time Moms

1. Prepare Your Mind

Your Whole Life Will Change

So let me put it to you straight. Whether you planned your pregnancy or it "just happened", being a Mom will change your life. Your entire life. I'm sure you've heard this before, just as you're hearing it from me now. You probably won't totally understand it until you're holding your child in your arms and have taken care of him or her for the first few weeks. Still, I'll try to explain. Your life without children is free and your responsibilities are based on what you need and what needs to be done to maintain your life and needs. When you bring a child into your life, you still need to take care of yourself, yes. But your main priority is making sure your child has everything he or she needs and is safe. For example, in your life without a child, if you have some extra money or want to do something special for yourself you may go get your nails or hair done. With a child, there may not be extra money. Or if there is, you'll probably spend it on your little one instead of yourself. A mom usually does (and should) think about what her child needs before herself. You will start thinking this way when your child is born, but you should start rearranging the way you think now so it will be an easier transition.

Think About Who You Allow In Your Life

Not only should you start to think differently about financial priorities, but about who you allow in your life, and now your child's life. Childless, you have only yourself to think about when choosing what relationships you allow in your life. When I say relationships, I mean romantic and otherwise. If you're single and pregnant, now is not the time to start a new romantic relationship. Now is the time to focus on being ready for your child. If you're already in a relationship with the baby's father (your boyfriend or husband), make sure that you have open communication with him about how you're going to parent your child together. Also, fix any problems you have in your relationship because your relationship problems will affect your child's life. If you have any friends or family who you know aren't good for you or are negative about the baby, keep them at a distance or let them know that you don't want any negativity in your life and around your child. Any close unhealthy relationships in your life can affect your child by causing him or her stress and can even delay development.

Don't Stress

Bringing a child into the world is going to change your life, yes, but don't stress yourself out! There will be less time for yourself. There is a whole other life to consider, yes. But you still need to take care of yourself. In order to be a good mom, you do need to make sure you're healthy too. Whatever stress you're dealing with will affect your child too. Being organized with your time will help to decrease stress. Taking time for yourself will also be important. Even a five minute break can center you and refocus your mind. You may find yourself hiding in the bathroom at some point in time to get a breather! Some good ways to destress are taking a walk (with or without your baby), sitting down and drinking a cup of hot tea, or reading a book for five or ten minutes.

2. Take Care Of Your Body

Take Care Of Yourself

Pregnancy takes your body through a lot. If you're planning to get pregnant, start getting your body in the best shape possible now. If you're already pregnant, you'll be limited in what exercises you can do, but still take care of yourself and do what you can do. Definitely ask your doctor what's safe. You want your body to be strong and prepared for the birth.

Exercise

Like I said, if you're already pregnant, there will be limited exercises you can do. Especially if you're a beginner exerciser. Moving your body and being fit will still be important. If you can do nothing else, walking is always a good option. Swimming is low impact and is good for pregnant women. It can be done at any stage of pregnancy. There are other options, but again, make sure you ask your doctor what's safe for you. Especially if you have health risks. After giving birth, the time to wait to begin exercise again is usually six weeks. You'll want to start doing safe exercises as soon as possible to get your body back into shape so that you can keep up with that little one! You may not have as much energy after delivery, and getting into an exercise routine will help your body get its strength back, as well as lose any extra baby weight. Of course, what you're putting into your body is important too...

Diet

Exercising to stay in shape is important, but it goes hand in hand with your diet. When you're a new mom, what you eat is more important. The importance of eating for energy becomes more evident. If you eat too much junk food, you will notice! Recovering from the pregnancy and delivery and at the same time, adjusting to having a new baby can take a toll on your body. You need to continue taking vitamins. Make sure that you make time to eat enough. And make what you do eat count! Include vegetables and leafy greens in your diet like broccoli, kale, spinach, and carrots. When you go shopping, check out the produce section and try new vegetables you haven't tried or didn't like before. Also, eat protein sources like chicken breast, eggs, Greek yogurt and beans. Calcium is one of the most important minerals for women to pay attention to, so drink milk and eat yogurt or cheese. If you don't eat dairy, try alternative calcium sources like soy milk, or take a calcium supplement. Finally, after grocery shopping, don't be afraid to try something new in the kitchen! When your little one grows into a toddler, you're going to need to try new dishes for his or her little taste buds anyway!

Pampering Yourself

As a mom, no one is going to take care of you more than you can take care of yourself. No, pampering yourself is not frivolous, either! It's important for your mental well being, as well as your physical well being. After all of that washing and sanitizing, put lotion on your hands. Wear a pretty scent you enjoy. Buy yourself a new nail polish. Light a candle and enjoy a few minutes of a book or drink some tea or coffee. Or wear some nice lacy underwear under your mom clothes. These are just a few examples of pampering yourself, but you can come up with some of your own, based off of what you enjoy.

3. Change Your Priorities

Getting Into A Routine

You're not number one anymore! This can take some getting used to. At the newborn stage of your child's life, you may feel like you don't even have time to take a shower some days. All of the appointments you need to keep, being up late hours of the night feeding, washing dirty baby clothes, preparing bottles, etc. Taking care of a newborn takes up most of your time. Getting into a routine will help you to stay sane as well as stay on track with everything that needs to be done. If you're lucky enough to have someone to help you the first few weeks, good for you. Not everyone does, but that can definitely be an advantage. As you're learning your baby, try to set the same time of day for washing and filling bottles, laundry, nap time and bed time.

First Time Mom

Your New Obligations

Being that you have more to do on a daily basis, you may need to learn to say no and cut some things out of your life. Before you welcome your child into the world, it's easier to fit fun activities such as date nights and time with friends into your schedule, but with a child, especially a newborn, it's not so convenient. You'll be staying home with your child a lot. Finding a babysitter isn't always so easy. For the first few weeks, you should keep your baby home in order not to expose him or her to extra germs and sick people anyway. Also, there will probably be a lot of people who want to visit and see the new addition to your family. Let some of them know that you don't want visitors for the time being. You're just getting your family adjusted to having a new little one and don't need extra company to entertain.

Remember To Stay Positive

So you're giving your baby the majority of your time, and your body is healing at the same time. It's easy to be stressed with everything going on. Keep it in your mind that your baby is a blessing and a positive addition to your life! Being a mother is not an easy job, but it's rewarding and helps you see what's most important in life.

4. Get Ready To Change Your Schedule

Get A Planner Or Calendar

To be successful and to make the most out of your time as a mom, you need to have a good schedule. I strongly suggest having a planner or calendar where you plan what you're doing with your time and for taking notes. To make it fun, pick one that's cute and fits your personality. Even go and get hilighters to mark the most important points. If you choose a calendar, hang it in a place where you'll always see it. Write down every doctor appointment, mark down feeding times, family events you need to remember, even grocery lists and lists of household chores that need to be done. Your planner will be like a reference to keep track of your time.

Planning Ahead

Your schedule will be different if you're working than if you're a stay at home mom, but is important either way. Have a plan for your days from start to finish. Plan what time you'll get up. Make sure it's before you know your child will wake up so that you'll have time to shower, get dressed and get your focus. You'll have time to pray or meditate if that's a part of your life, and write look over your schedule to see what you have planned for the day. Also, it will be so much easier for you to shower and get dressed by yourself than when your little one is already awake and demanding your attention. Getting up earlier may be forfeiting a little sleep, but your day will go so much better.

Your Diaper Bag

A really important part of preparing for your days will be your diaper bag. Leaving the house with your baby unprepared can be very inconvenient. Keeping the diaper bag ready with everything in it, kept in the same spot can make things go smoother when you're getting ready to take baby out. Some essentials you'll need to keep in there will be diapers, baby wipes, an extra change of clothes, prepared bottles, a toy to keep your little one busy, snacks for an older baby or toddler, and a cloth to wipe any spit up.

5. Buying Baby Items

Where Your Baby Will Sleep

One of your biggest purchases you'll make for your baby is going to be a crib. There are different options you have for where your baby will sleep. A lot of cribs nowadays are designed for the stages of life. The crib stage, when your baby is first born and through the first year. It will convert into a toddler bed when your baby is ready, then into a big kid bed. There's also the option of buying a bassinet for your newborn. It takes up less space, but can only be used for a few months, until your little one is too big for it. Something that you'll need, whether your baby sleeps in it or not, is a pack and play. A pack and play is a portable play pen that you can put your baby in during the day to play in and stay safe while you're busy and watching close by. This can also be where he or she sleeps. You can choose this option if you're trying to conserve space or for travel. It can be folded up when not in use and taken with you if you're spending the night somewhere besides home with baby. The choice is yours, just make sure that baby is safe wherever he or she is sleeping. It is not a good idea to have your baby sleep in bed with you.

Diapers And Wipes

This will be your biggest expense! It's a good idea to stock up. If you're planning on having a baby shower, you'll probably get a lot if there are a good number of people coming. If you want to, instead of a baby shower, you can throw a diaper party. Just cook some food and invite friends and family over, asking them to bring diapers for the baby. It's not important to buy all one brand. What is important is that when you stock up or have people buy them, that different sizes are purchased. When baby comes, pay attention to how he or she reacts to the diapers. If your little one gets a rash from one brand of diapers, don't buy those ones anymore! Same goes for baby wipes. Your best bet is getting unscented baby wipes.

Bottles

Unless you're exclusively breast feeding and you're not storing milk (it's all coming straight from you to your baby), you're going to need to buy bottles. There are so many different brands and types of bottles, so I suggest that you go shopping and look around. See what your options are. The most important thing will be the nipple on the bottle and whether your baby is taking the milk from it. The same with a pacifier. If you buy different pacifiers, you'll soon know which one is your little one's favorite.

Clothes

When buying clothes for your baby, keep in mind how quickly your baby will grow. So you may not want to go out and buy the most expensive clothes you can find for your baby. I know you'll want to get some cute things for your little one. That's natural. So why not buy a special outfit for each holiday? If you have family members who have older kids and have left over baby clothes they won't use again, they may want to hand them down to you.

Car Seat And Stroller

With both a car seat and stroller, you have so many to choose from. Again, I suggest that you look at your options. Go online and research what's out there. Even go in the stores and see what they have. Choose which is right for you. Keep in mind that most hospitals will want to check that your car seat is safe before letting you take the baby home with it. You may want to ask to make sure.

Other Items

There are so many extra baby items out there on the market that you won't necessarily need but may want to consider A couple of them include baby bottle sanitizers and baby wipe warmers. Part of the fun of preparing for baby is shopping!

6. Your Support System

First Time Mom

A good support system will be a big help to you when you have your baby. Knowing who to call and who to trust when you need someone to watch your child is valuable. It will help you to stay sane as a busy mother, and will be a benefit to your child. Your support system doesn't have to be huge either. If you get overwhelmed and need some rest or need to go somewhere important where you can't take your child with you, have at least one or two people you can call.

When you think of all of the people you know, you can come up with all of the people you know that you'd trust to watch your child. Whether it's your mom or dad, sister or brother, best friend, or your neighbor who you've known for years. Before the baby is even here, go to each one of the people you trust and want to be a part of your support system. Let them know that you would like them to be a part of your child's life. Ask them if they'd be available to watch your child at times. Find out what their schedules are. After the conversation you have with each person you want to be a part of your support system, if they are good fit to be a baby sitter, write their name, phone number and address in your planner.

Knowing who you're going to call when you need someone to watch your little one, and even who you're going to call when you need some new mother advice is another way to be prepared going into motherhood. If you go through your mental Rolodex and can't think of anyone you would trust with your child, find people! For support as a mother, there are so many different forums and support groups to be a part of where women come together and have created their own community. Google "mom support group forums online" and there are many places online that you'll find to be a solace to you. Another option you have if you'd rather meet people face to face is to join a group for mothers in your community. Ask your local hospital, church, or community center about groups there are for mothers in your area. A big plus is that usually, there will be childcare at a support group for mothers.

7. Welcoming Your Little One

The Hospital

After all of the preparation you've done changing your priorities, getting mentally and physically ready for baby and buying baby items, now comes the time to welcome your new baby into your home. First, lets talk about the hospital. Make sure that you bring the car seat to the hospital when you go in to deliver. Also, make sure that you pack a bag for yourself and the baby. Include a change of clothes for yourself and a robe. Put socks, clean underwear and a pair of slippers in your bag. Remember a camera for pictures. You'll want to capture those first moments of life. For the baby, pack an outfit for him or her to go home in. Also, bring a baby blanket. You won't need to bring diapers because the hospital with will supply you with them during your stay.

Your House

Before you go into labor, set up your baby's bedroom. Put the crib together. Set up the dresser and put away any clothes you have for him or her. If you have a changing table, set that up too. Also, clean the house so that it's freshly sanitized. That way, you won't be frantically cleaning when you bring your new baby home and he or she won't get sick from any left over germs. Another good idea is having meals prepared for the first couple of weeks. Even freeze some things that you can thaw so that the food will last for two or three weeks. That is, if you don't have anyone to help you by bringing over anything. It will just make the transition welcoming your little one into your home that much easier.

Utilizing Your Support System

First Time Mom

Let certain people on your list of people to call know when you go into the hospital to deliver. That way, they can plan to come and help you when you bring your baby home. Like I said earlier on, don't invite everybody over the first few weeks. You don't want too many people in your house when you're adjusting to having your baby home. Just one or two people who will be helping out. Helping you prepare meals or clean. Maybe watching the baby while you get some rest to recover from delivery.

Enjoy Your Baby!

After preparing for your baby and welcoming him or her into your home, you're adjusting to a new way of life. Don't forget to enjoy every stage! Time goes by and your little one will grow so quickly. Enjoy the spitting up, changing diapers and late nights up putting him or her back to sleep just as much as the cuteness. Soon, he or she will be in the toddler stage and you'll be dealing with potty training. Enjoy it all! You only get one chance at them being small. So make the most of it!

First Time Mom
Conclusion

Having a new baby is an exciting and stressful time for many. From all of the symptoms you will experience physically to all of the emotions you will experience that will mentally weigh on you, there is a lot you will go through. It is important that you brace yourself for everything that is to come.

Having this audio guidebook is a great way to recognize what symptoms are normal, and which are alarming. You can also prepare yourself for each trimester, and ensure that you are taking the best possible care of yourself. Even though pregnancy is a largely physical experience, you should also do your best to slow down and enjoy it. This may not be easy, especially if you are experiencing difficult symptoms or a high-risk pregnancy, but it is important since this experience is one you only get to have once in a lifetime.

It is important that you prepare yourself for childbirth well in advance, and that you maintain open lines of communication with everyone involved. The more open you are and honest you are about how you are feeling, the easier this process will be for you.

Most importantly, stay calm and relaxed as much as possible, and nurture yourself in every way that you can to make this process as easy and as comfortable for you and your baby as possible.

Thank you.

SLEEP LITTLE BABY: THE ROCK-A-BYE BABY SOLUTION FOR MODERN PARENT

Raising a Baby Doesn't Have to Be so Hard! Learn the Best Kept Secrets of Baby Sleep and Enjoy That Long Gone Rested Feeling Again.

Table of Contents

Introduction 113

Chapter 1: A Healthy Sleep Cycle for Your Baby 114

Chapter 2: What Is The Sleep Training Solution? 123

Chapter 3: Babies and Their Sleep Cycles 129

Chapter 4: Why Is Your Baby Crying? 134

Chapter 5: Minimize Sleep Disruptors 144

Chapter 6: How To Use Simple Steps To Help Your Kids Sleep In 48 Hours 152

Chapter 7: Importance Of Establishing A Good Bedtime Routine . 161

Chapter 8: Sleep Solutions and Strategies 165

Chapter 9: More Health Tips for Mother and Child 173

Chapter 10: Analyze 188

Chapter 11: Teaching Your Baby the Art of Sleeping 193

Chapter 12: Safety 199

Conclusion 204

Sleep Little Baby
Introduction

Whether you are a new parent or a parent-to-be I created this audiobook just for you. I struggled getting my first child to sleep and nap consistently. My husband and I were exhausted and at our wits end. I vowed if I ever found a method, tip or trick that worked I would share it with every parent I knew so that they could experience a good night's rest.

I'm actually the least likely person to be making an audiobook like this as I'm not a doctor and I don't have a professional background. However, I do have a drive and determination to share all I have learned through researching countless articles, books, and blogs, talking with physicians, pediatricians, and several specialists in the field to bring you the tips and techniques in this book.

I have tried to cover a wide range of conditions and "what if" scenarios to give you the best options known to man for helping you and your little one get the rest you need and deserve. Please keep in mind that not every method will work for every child and what worked for the first may not work for the second or third. The important thing to remember is to keep adjusting the techniques you use as your child grows and learns. You are sure to find many practical and proven tips in this handy guide, so jump right in and start learning today so you can get your rest tonight.

Thanks again for purchasing this audiobook, I hope you enjoy it!

Chapter 1: A Healthy Sleep Cycle for Your Baby

What to Expect

After the excitement of a new baby dies down the real work of parenting begins. If you are a new parent then chances are you've been inundated with well-wishers and many with good intentions, each wanting with all their heart to help you. This however, is one of the first tasks you'll have to do as a parent, to sift through all the chaff and come up with a parenting plan that will create a family dynamic that will benefit everyone.

Unfortunately, this is not always easy to do. Just keep in mind that you have three main objectives to accomplish in those first few days with your baby.

1) to get to know your little one. Yes, he or she already has a personality and believe it or not a mind a mind of her own. It is up to you to learn and understand her needs, wants, and expectations.

2) to reinforce the person that is trusting you with their lives. You want your baby to feel safe and cared for. Even at this early stage what you do to reinforce their sense of security can benefit that child for years to come.

3) to enjoy your new role as a parent. There will be times when you will be so exhausted that you won't be able to think straight. There will be times when you won't have a clue what your baby wants. These times can be discouraging, especially when it's 3:00 in the morning and the incessant crying seems to never end but if you use those times to remember the joys of parenthood you'll have a better chance of plowing your way through those rough nights.

The manner in which you and your baby connect can actually influence every aspect of that child's life, not just his or her sleeping patterns so the sooner you decide what type of relationship the two of you will have the sooner the baby will begin to adjust to life in this great big world. This means that you must educate yourself on what a

Sleep Little Baby

normal baby's sleep patterns should be so you will know when your baby' sleeping schedule is out of whack.

So, what is a normal sleep pattern for a newborn baby? It goes without saying that they will be sleeping a lot. There is a lot of energy expended in being born and the first few days they will be pretty exhausted and in need of rest. According to the babycenter.com, there is nothing unusual about a newborn sleeping as much as 16 to 17 hours a day. The biggest challenge for many parents is that they tend to wake-up at the most inopportune times, at which point their needs must be tended to. This translates into an extremely irregular sleep pattern and a limited amount of sleep for you.

Birth to six weeks: Newborns tend to have unpredictable sleep patterns, which are much shorter than what older children or adults are accustomed to but there is a reason for this. Unlike adults, much of a baby's sleep time is spent in the REM stage (rapid eye movement). This stage is believed to be essential for enhancing the development of their little brains. Still, it can be frustrating when you can't seem to get your REM sleep because your babies REM stage is so short. The good news is that in healthy babies, this stage usually starts to get longer at about six weeks of age.

Six to eight weeks: At around six weeks of age, babies tend to have discerned the difference between day and night. It is at this point that they will naturally begin to adjust their sleep cycles taking shorter naps during the daylight hours and start a longer sleep routine during the night. You can encourage this routine by following some very basic steps in the family routine that will help the baby to understand when it is time to sleep.

Four to six months: At four months, most babies have stretched out their sleeping cycle to at least eight hours and some have managed to sleep through a full twelve hours. While some babies reach this stage earlier (at around two months) most do not reach this milestone until sometime after the four-month marker.

Sleep Little Baby

Simple Strategies to Help Babies Learn a Sleeping Schedule

It is important to note that even healthy babies will have trouble slipping into a regular sleeping routine, which can make it very hard for the parents to maintain a consistent schedule. However, there are a few things that can help the baby to acclimate to a more normal sleep cycle. In training your baby to know when to sleep try these simple strategies:

1. In the first few weeks, most babies will only be awake for an hour or two at a stretch. Encourage sleep by making it easy for them to take regular naps. It may seem counterproductive to encourage sleep but if the baby is kept awake for longer than their natural cycle they can become over-stimulated and then it will be more difficult for them to fall asleep naturally.

2. Teach them the difference between night and day. In the daytime keep the room bright and let as much light in as possible. Allow your home to fill with natural noises heard through the day and play and interact with your little one as much as possible. When darkness falls, dim the lights and play soothing music for your baby. The house should be as peaceful as possible and resist the temptation to play with them. This will encourage a more regular sleep pattern and before long the baby will learn to distinguish that daytime is for activity and nighttime for resting on his own.

3. Follow your baby's cues. Babies may not be able to speak but they do know how to let you know when they need something. Look for the different signs they give when they are tired. Watch for the rubbing of the eyes, pulling the ears, and that tell-tale sign of irritability when all their needs are met.

Benefits of Healthy Sleep

Most parents fully expect that in the first few months of a baby's arrival that they are going to lose a lot of sleep. It starts with the feeding times every two or three hours and moves on to answering the baby's cries at all hours throughout the night and day. This routine is perfectly normal in the first few weeks but if you find that your baby is still struggling to sleep through longer stretches of time as they grow older, it is something that needs to be addressed. There are many good reasons why babies need to have good quality sleep in their lives.

You've probably already seen what happens when your baby doesn't get enough sleep. One of the first things you'll notice is that it actually disrupts their attention span, which can have a negative effect on their lives in many ways. Consider these points:

It inhibits their ability to learn. From the time your child enters the world a learning process begins. For your baby's brains to mature they need to be able to sleep well. Studies have shown that those babies that receive higher quality sleep during the night developed better cognitively.

It retards their development. Aside from the impact lack of sleep has on the brain and its ability to learn, prolonged sleep deprivation in your baby could result in other developmental issues. Studies have shown that many children suffering from ADHD did not get enough sleep when they were younger. There is also some concern that this condition could lead to obesity, diabetes, and other serious medical conditions.

With all these things in mind, it is very important that every child no matter what age is able to get an adequate supply of sleep every day. It's is okay to miss a day or two of sleep; it happens to everyone but concern should be that these occasional nights without sleep do not become a pattern that will lead to problems they may have to deal with for the rest of their lives.

What is Healthy Baby Sleep?

Babies are notorious for changing sleep cycles, waking in the night, restlessness, and inconsolable crying. To some, these behaviors may seem erratic or random. However, there are important reasons why your baby sleeps (or doesn't sleep) in the way that she does.

Understanding how baby sleep works is the first step towards giving your baby the healthy sleep she needs for proper development—and to getting back some sleep of your own!

Sleep Little Baby

The first question to ask is, what does healthy baby sleep look like?

Healthy baby sleep is more than just getting 'enough' sleep overall, although that is important. Healthy baby sleep also means sleep of the right quality and at the right times. Understanding all that goes into these factors is an enigma to many, but we're here to break it down for you! It all starts by understanding how baby sleep works.

You've no doubt noticed by now that babies change rapidly. As your baby grows, his or her sleep also changes to accommodate development. While every baby is different, there are age-based norms that can help you to understand your baby's changing sleep patterns.

Check out the following table to get an idea of how much sleep your baby needs according to age. Keep in mind that these numbers are averages. Your baby's sleep needs will likely fall within these ranges, but if they seem to need more or less sleep than other babies, it may simply mean that your baby has different sleep needs. If in doubt, speak with your pediatrician.

Keep the following age-specific tips for bedtime:

Newborns

Newborns may go to bed quite late, anywhere from 7pm – 11pm. Their brains have not yet learned to produce melatonin in conjunction with circadian rhythms, so bedtime may not be related to the dark and may not always happen at the same time. Trying to get them to a consistent, early bedtime is good, however, your newborn probably won't be ready for highly structured sleep schedules until closer to 3 months.

3 Months – 18 Months

From 3 months, it's time to start training your baby to have a consistent, early bedtime. We'll be going over some great tips and strategies for sleep training later in this book, but for now, know that you will want to aim for a bedtime around 7pm.

18 Months – 36 Months

Sleep Little Baby

As your baby gets older and enters the toddler stage, she will be able to stay up a little later...but not much! Babies in this age range do best with a bedtime between 7 and 8:30.

Don't forget that healthy sleep depends on more than just the amount of sleep your baby gets. Another important factor is your baby's sleep cycles, which reflect the quality of your baby's sleep.

It's not unusual for adults to fall asleep soon after they close their eyes. An adult sleep cycle includes time spent in deep sleep and in REM sleep. The length of the cycle varies depending on whether it is the first, second, or later cycle of the night, but on average lasts between 90 and 120 minutes.

Babies' sleep cycles are similar to adults' in that they involve both deep sleep and REM sleep. However, it takes babies much longer to fall asleep once their eyes are closed. Their cycles are also much shorter, often lasting less than an hour and rarely more than 90 minutes. It's important for your baby to experience complete sleep cycles in order to get the quality of rest they need for proper development.

In addition to quantity and quality of baby sleep, we should also consider timing. Babies don't sleep only at night, and when a baby sleeps plays an important role in preventing tiredness. For babies, daytime sleep is just as important as nighttime sleep.

Newborns sleep often throughout the day and night, and may not exhibit any specific napping pattern. Newborns should be allowed to sleep whenever they need to. Although you can take steps to start developing routines with your newborn, this is not the time to begin hard-core sleep training. Newborns may start to consolidate their napping periods as early as six weeks, and should be ready for more structured sleep training around 3 months.

20 Facts About Baby Sleep

Now that we've gone over the big-picture factors that influence healthy baby sleep, here are 20 important facts that you need to know:

Sleep Little Baby

Your baby's clock is off. Most babies don't develop their own circadian rhythms until about 12 weeks old. As a result, melatonin isn't produced in response to darkness the way that it is for you and me. This is one of the reasons that newborn infants sleep on and off around the clock.

Babies like to be close. Many babies find it comforting to sleep close their mothers. This includes both co-sleeping and simply sleeping in the same room as mom. Both have potential advantages for your baby's quality of sleep.

Your soothing could be stimulating. Sometimes a parent's efforts to soothe their baby has the opposite effect. Common examples include wrapping a baby too snuggly in their blanket, talking to them when they're trying to fall asleep, or picking them up every time they make noise in their sleep.

Babies need bedtimes. Routine is helpful for most people, regardless of age, and babies are no different. Babies who are put down for naps around the same time every day tend to fall asleep more easily and wake up less often.

Babies need a change of routine as they grow. The sleep schedule of a newborn will differ from that of a six-month-old or an eight-month-old. Understanding how much sleep babies need at different ages, and how often they need it, will help you to create effective routines for maximizing your baby's healthy sleep.

Babies need to unwind before bed time. Too much stimulus before bed can make it hard for a baby to fall asleep. Choose evening rituals that soothe, rather than stimulate.

Babies like to practice. When babies are learning to sit up, roll over, or crawl, they may wake up in the night to practice these skills. They will often put themselves back to sleep, so avoid further interrupting their sleep by picking babies up unnecessarily.

Babies have short sleep cycles. While the average adult sleep cycle lasts 90-120 minutes, a baby's sleep cycles is usually only 40-60 minutes.

Sleep Little Baby

Teething hurts. Babies who are teething wake up more easily due to painful gum irritation.

Babies don't like to be interrupted. Noises and squirming are normal parts of baby sleep; there's usually no need to intervene for these kinds of disruptions.

Your baby is too tired. Overtired babies have a harder time falling asleep and staying asleep. The quality of sleep may also be reduced if your baby is fatigued.

Babies like to suck. Babies are biologically programmed to suck. Providing a breast, bottle, or pacifier will comfort and relax them before and during sleep.

Waking up at night is useful. The ability to wake up easily is an evolutionary advantage that helps babies get their needs taken care of. A poorly sleeping baby can be disheartening, but take comfort in knowing that waking up at night is meant to help keep your baby safe.

Babies need to move. Movement, such as carrying, bouncing, or rocking, can relieve digestive discomfort and muscle pain that keep babies awake.

Closed eyes don't mean deep sleep. Due to their shorter sleep cycles, babies may only be dozing when they appear to be sleeping.

Babies have tiny tummies. Food is processed quickly, and hunger can be painful. Newborn babies need to be fed 8-12 times in every 24 hour period, so they should not sleep through the night.

Babies experience discomfort. Gas, teething, hunger, and thirst are just a few of the common discomforts that babies face. Finding ways to relieve discomfort will help your baby get better sleep.

Babies are learning to self-soothe. Babies don't start out with the skills to soothe themselves. Crying is often the only tool they have to get their needs met. Your baby probably won't begin to learn to self soothe until after three months.

Sleep Little Baby

Sleep is important for development. Babies don't just need sleep to get over being tired. Good baby sleep also promotes healthy brain and nervous system development.

Light matters. Sleeping in the dark helps babies' bodies learn to produce melatonin, an important hormone for sleep regulation. Keeping the baby's room dark at night can help them as they develop their own circadian rhythms. On the other hand, having them nap in a dark room during the day may interfere with circadian rhythm, causing babies to wake up more often during the night.

As you can see, baby sleep is affected by a wide variety of factors!

With so many influences, it's no wonder that parents often feel overwhelmed when babies don't sleep well. The more you understand about your baby's sleep needs, the easier it will be to problem solve sleep issues. By taking the time to get a hold on the basics, you will have less stress and a much greater chance for success.

Chapter 2: What Is The Sleep Training Solution?

Sleep training is the way toward helping a baby to figure out alone how to get to sleep and stay asleep during the night.

Some infants do this faster and easier. But many others need help along the way. They have difficulty calming themselves down to sleep, or getting back to sleep when they've awake. In this book, we will try to share the mom's experience. We describe the main approaches to sleep training; we will discuss the existing literature as well as some new developments for 2017.

When can I begin sleep training with my baby?

Most specialists suggest starting when your child is between four and six months old. By around four months, babies have usually begun to build up a healthy sleep-wake cycle and dropped the most of their night feedings. These are signs they might be prepared to start sleep training. Many babies this age are developmentally able to sleep for long intervals during the evening.

Would that be valid in your situation? Your child is unique, and each baby is different. Some babies may not be ready for sleep training until they are older than six months. Some newborn babies sleep more than six or seven hours, while others won't start to do that until later.

You could ask your doctor if you are not sure if your baby is ready for sleep training yet or not.

How to prepare for sleep training - Step by step instructions

Recommendations to set the stage for sleep training successfully:

One of the most important tasks for parents is to have a sleep schedule. In reality, it is never too late to have and stick to the bedtime routine, but the most efficient will be when your baby is

Sleep Little Baby

around six weeks of age. A part of your routine can be a warm bath and soothing music.

- Timing is relevant for your success as well. You should be very consistent and STICK TO BEDTIME between seven and eight o'clock to avoid children getting over tired.

- Sticking to the predictable daytime schedule is another important factor. Try to get your baby up about the same time every morning. Feed him and put him down for rests at about the same times throughout the day. This routine helps him relax and feel secure, and a happy baby settles down to sleep much more quickly.

- Be sure that your child doesn't have any medical condition that could affect their sleep. It is paramount to address any underlying condition by your doctor.

What are the best sleep training options for me?

Every parent wanders which technique are the best in their situation. You can introduce healthy sleeping habits in many ways. You should understand many of them, and by testing, you should find which one is the most comfortable for you and your child.

You know that what works well for one child, will not necessary work for yours. Get ready to have some trial and error while figuring out an approach suitable for your family and situation.

You can always turn to experts who have written many books on the subject or listen to other parents' experience. Have a look at sleep training basics before you start.

The subject of training children to sleep is written in many books, and you can also find extensive research on the subject. As a result, the conclusions for parents are: "BE CONSISTENT! The training you pick MUST be the one you can stick with and follow through. Be flexible and observe your baby's reaction. If his mood and behavior change for the worse, consider stopping for a few weeks before picking another approach or try the same again."

Sleep Little Baby

Baby's Sleep Habits

Babies have different sleep patterns compared to adults. A lot of things can distract them and prevent from going to sleep. There are also lots of things that can disrupt their sleep, especially at night. Also, sleep habits change through the baby's first 12 months of life, making it more difficult to get them got to bed on a regular schedule.

Newborns typically sleep a lot. They sleep on an average of 16 to 17 hours each day. They sleep most of the day and through the night. However, some babies are less inclined to sleep- and stay asleep- for more than 2 to 4 hours during the 1st few weeks after birth. Some wake up frequently, crying and very irritable during the night. Parents lose sleep and become tired and irritable throughout the next day.

Sleep cycles are much shorter in babies compared to adults. Babies have lighter sleep and get disrupted more easily, too. This is because newborns spend more time in a sleep stage called REM (rapid eye movement). The REM stage of sleep is believed to be important during the newborn period and through the rest of infancy because it supports rapid brain development.

When the baby is 6 to 8 weeks old, sleep during the day is often reduced to short naps and nighttime sleep generally lasts longer at this age. Most babies would wake up night only to feed. REM stage is also shortened. Babies at this age generally spend longer periods in the non-REM stage of sleep, which is deeper and less easily disturbed.

At 3 months of age, babies sleep on an average of 15 hours. This includes both daytime naps and nighttime sleep.

By 4 to 6 months, babies generally are able to sleep through the night for 8 to 12 hours. Some babies reach this milestone in as early as 6 weeks old, but most do so by 5 months of age.

At 4 months of age, babies typically have started to adapt a fairly regular pattern of sleeping and waking hours. There is reduced waking up during the night for their nighttime feedings. Even with the sleep-wake pattern, this is not the time to impose rigid sleeping programs. The baby's pattern at this point would have been an adjustment to family life. The sleep/wake pattern is more likely in response to the general schedule of activities within the home.

What parents can do when the baby has started to display sleep/wake patterns is to try sleep training. Learn a few sleep training methods that can be used for this age. Observe how the baby reacts to the method and adjust accordingly. Parents should not force the baby to stick to a chosen method. Instead, parents should adjust their methods depending on the baby's response. Every baby responds in a unique way when it comes to sleep. If the baby shows any indication that he is not yet ready for sleep training, take a step back. Let the baby follow his own sleep patterns and techniques, then try sleep training again after a few weeks.

Between the ages of 4 to 6 months, most babies are now able to sleep through the night. Waking up for nighttime feedings becomes less frequently as the baby grows older. Sleeping through the night now means sleeping 8 to 12 hours straight, without waking up for feedings or need for a diaper change. This is good news for parents, as they get more sleep at night, too.

Some babies, however, are still unable to sleep for 8 hours straight. A lot of babies still have to wake up frequently for nighttime feedings. This is normal. Remember that babies have their own unique sleeping patterns and reach certain milestones at different rates.

It is also normal for babies who have been regularly sleeping through the night to return to waking up frequently again. This does not indicate that something is wrong. More likely, the baby is becoming more socially aware. The baby waking up is more because of the need for the parents' company.

How to Establish Good Sleep Habits

Establishing good sleeping habits should start as early as possible. It does not mean training the baby at a very young age. Establishing good sleep habits means promoting a consistent sleep schedule and helping the baby associate sleep as a secure, comforting and desirable activity.

Recognizing signs

Parents should be aware of the signs that the baby is sleepy and cater to the need in a timely manner. Waiting too long before putting the baby to sleep will make him too tired and sleep will be more difficult. They should act on these signs immediately by promoting an environment conducive for sleep.

A few common signs that the baby is ready for sleep include:

- rubs or brings his hands over his eyes
- flicks or brings his hand to his ear
- appearance of faint, dark circles under the baby's eyes
- becomes more fussy than usual
- Easily irritated- baby cries and whines at the slightest provocation
- blankly stares into space
- Frequently stretches and yawns
- loses interest in his environment, such as in people and toys, and turns away
- Increasingly turns quiet and lies still
- Buries face into the parent's (or caregiver's) chest

Teaching day and night

As early as 2 weeks old, parent can start teaching babies to differentiate day from night. Associate different activities for day and night. For example, during the day, keep the room bright. Interact with the baby a lot, such as talking and playing more often. Let the baby hear regular daytime household noise such as music, phones and sounds of household appliances running like TVs and dishwashers. Wake him up if he tends to fall asleep during his daytime feedings. At night, spend less time with active play. Start to minimize household noise. Turn down music or the TV. Also, turn the lights down low. Over time, the baby will figure out that active play and noisy environments are for daytime. Low lights and quiet environments will denote "night" and a transition time for sleep.

Start a bedtime routine

Babies learn by association and through repeated experiences. Take advantage of this by initiating bedtime rituals. Baths, changing clothes, and lullabies are simple ways to start a bedtime routine.

Chapter 3: Babies and Their Sleep Cycles

It is an undeniable fact that having a newborn in the house can wreak havoc on the sleep patterns and schedules of new parents. Staying awake may lead to increased crankiness, but it generally has little long-term health effects. Babies are like little snowflakes, every one of them has different traits that may affect how much physical activity they like, how long they sleep at night, and how much they cry as a whole. Typical babies are usually quite self-soothing; they have a schedule for sleeping and feeding and usually fall asleep on their own. However, do not be quick to blame yourself or feel discouraged if you have an atypical baby who is less self-soothing. As a parent, there are many things you can do and many methods you can try to help your little angel sleep better at night.

States and Stages of Sleep

Babies' sleep patterns change as they age. Though the stages of sleep are pretty basic, actually getting a child to sleep may require certain adjustments and foresight. While many veteran parents may already know this, sometimes a refresher is needed. Additionally, first-time parents and parents adopting either their first child or a child of a different age than their other children should find the following information very useful as it is sorted by age. In the beginning, a lot of observation is required. Despite this, you can start setting up a schedule and adjust your plan as your child's needs change. So let's take a closer look at sleep regulation and how it affects both babies and adults.

For most, sleep is regulated by outward stimuli (i.e. light and dark surroundings, noise levels, etc.) The circadian biological clock rhythms have not yet been developed at any level for children less than 6 months old. For adults, the internal circadian rhythm can be affected by whether or not they are a morning or evening person, so consider yourself as well when attempting to identify your child's sleep habits. Many people argue strongly for genetics and the nature versus nurture argument, so it is worth mentioning that if you are an evening person, then either by genetics or by your own habits rubbing off on your child, you may start to notice that your child has likes and dislikes similar to your own when it comes to sleeping.

Not only does the body's internal circadian biological clock regulate sleeping patterns, but there is also the additional involvement of sleep/wake homeostasis. Your internal circadian biological clock responds to signals sent throughout the body by a group of cells in the hypothalamus gland called the suprachiasmatic nucleus (SCN). Once these cells respond to the surrounding dark or light received through the optic nerve in the eyes, they signal other parts of the brain to start waking you up or making you feel sleepy. When there is light and the other parts of the brain are signaled to wake you, cortisol and other hormone levels are raised, melatonin and similar hormones are lowered, and the temperature of your body rises. It is the opposite when it is dark and you are going to sleep. These are the settings you want your baby to have in the future.

Next, we will take a closer look at how children sleep according to age.

Newborns (1-2 months old)

Sleep is the main activity for a newborn, followed closely by feedings and diaper changes. On average, a newborn sleeps between 11 and 18 hours a day when all the time is added up. The clock governing your infant's sleep-wake times is set by need. While asleep, their faces, arms, and legs may twitch; they may smile, attempt to suck their fists or thumbs, and may generally be a bit wiggly even while they sleep. When it is time for a nap, babies will express their need for rest in many ways. And with a bit of extended observation, you too can learn your baby's indicators.

Fussing, yawning, crying, and rubbing their eyes are classic sleepy indicators. For the best results, it is best to put your baby to bed when they display signs of sleepiness rather than putting them to bed after they have already fallen asleep in your arms. This directly ties into self-soothing, which tends to be easier when your baby is close enough to sleep. By putting a newborn to bed when they are extremely sleepy — as opposed to when they are already asleep — your baby will fall asleep quicker and much more reliably.

Furthermore, a newborn will nap at intervals throughout the day, regardless, but by exposing them to more light, sound, and playful attention during the day, their bodies will begin to associate the dimmer, quieter environment of the evening with the reduction in activity. These steps are the groundwork that encourage more nighttime sleep and more restful nights for all.

In brief then, the best tip for starting sleep training with your newborn is to simply observe signs of sleepiness which will allow you to put your baby in their crib before they actually fall asleep. Lay your baby on their back to sleep without any blankets, pillows, or soft items near their head. And once again, encourage your baby to sleep more at night by exposing them to more activity, light, and sounds during the day and by significantly reducing those things during the night at established times.

Infants (3-11 months old)

Between the ages of 3 and 11 months, your infant's nighttime feeding requirements should begin to taper off. By 4 months, your baby should be able to sleep for at least 4 to 5 hours straight. And in most cases, nighttime feedings are no longer a necessity by 6 months of age. At this age, your baby should be sleeping throughout the night as well as napping 1 to 4 times a day, with an average time that ranges between 30 minutes long for more frequent naps and 2 hours long during minimal naps. There are keys to maintaining this successfully. Infants typically need 9 to 12 hours' worth of sleep per night.

Once again, place your baby in their crib when they show that they are sleepy rather than after they fall asleep for both naps and bedtime. Be sure to keep their bedding area friendly and stable, and get a good night light that gives off just the right amount of dim light to see but not enough to keep the baby awake — and be sure to keep it in the same spot. Also, place the baby monitor in an ideal location as opposed to moving it around too often. Remember, consistent stability is key.

Be wary of accidentally setting up inhibiting routines like always rocking your baby to sleep. A standard bedtime routine would typically include dinner, a bath, placing the baby in a comfortable sleeper, and then putting him or her to bed. It is incredibly important that your baby learn to self-soothe. A baby with a standard sleeping schedule who is a self-soother will make it easier to pinpoint irregularities and find out whether something is wrong. If your baby is usually asleep at a particular time and starts to fidget or becomes increasingly uncomfortable, it can be easier to pinpoint social, developmental, or health concerns. When babies feel ill, they are more likely to experience disrupted sleep. Now is the perfect time to establish a regular bedtime routine if you have not already done so. And for those of you who have, just keep at it. It is the best way to go.

Toddlers (1-3 years old)

Overall, toddlers need an average of 13 hours of sleep per day. When your baby reaches 18 months, they should be down to one nap that lasts between 1 to 3 hours long. It is important that this nap be taken early in the afternoon to avoid any issues with bedtime. At this age, toddlers may begin to resist going to bed. They may have nightmares or wake up and fight not to go back to sleep. And the fact that they can now get up and walk around as they please also makes it more difficult to keep them in bed.

Thus, during this stage, it is incredibly important to maintain the sleep schedule as rigorously as possible. The bedtime schedule can now include a soothing song or story. Keep the layout and design of the bedroom that your toddler sleeps in the same each night. The inclusion of a security object, like a special stuffed animal or blanket, can make a big difference in keeping your toddler in bed as well. Enforce the bedtime routine nightly, and if it should become necessary, add in an early daytime nap schedule to aid your toddler in being tired by bedtime.

Differentiating Between Sleepy Signs and Fatigue Signs

Knowing when to take a newborn to their crib becomes easier once you familiarize yourself with specific baby sleep signs. When you see your baby yawning, rubbing their eyes, or fussing, it is time to take them to their crib — the ultimate place for them to sleep. Other signs include decreased activity, being less vocal, being quieter, displaying slower motions, and eyelids drooping.

However, sometimes you may think that your baby needs sleep and so you take them to their crib only to find out that they will not go to sleep. This usually happens when parents misinterpret the signs of fatigue for sleep signals. Your little one is fatigued if you see him or her rubbing their eyes, fussing and being cranky, or becoming overtired. This is not the time to take them to their crib, but it requires taking other measures first. However, if the initial efforts aren't bearing any fruit, it is time to look for a more sophisticated and effective method to help your baby be a self-soother. They really need your help here.

Chapter 4: Why Is Your Baby Crying?

Babies are adorable little creatures. They are stress-relievers. When you're exhausted from work and you see your baby smile, it takes away all your fatigue. What a baby does is bring colors to your world. Suddenly, life has meaning. She is your reason for living. Although it can be blissful raising a baby, it is tedious to put them to sleep. Many parents struggle with it. If you have a baby who cries a lot and finds it extremely hard to fall asleep, you may want to find out why. You would be able to resolve the problem once you understand why your baby is crying. This list will help you find out the reason why your baby cries.

Your baby may be hungry. Hunger is almost always the culprit why a baby cries. That's how she communicates that she wants to be fed. Try to remember the last time you fed her milk and if it's about time to feed her again. Watch out for other signs like a baby sucking her finger. That's a sure sign your baby is hungry.

Your baby wants to sleep. Another reason why babies cry is simply because they want to sleep and they aren't comfortable with their position. Some babies sleep when their mothers carry them. Some sleep with a background music on. It is different for every baby. Once you figure this out, your life becomes easier.

Your baby doesn't want a dirty diaper. Perhaps she has been wearing it for hours and it needs to be changed. Or your baby may have pooped on her diaper. Sometimes the only solution is to change. Once you do, your baby will usually stop crying.

Your baby wants you to carry her. Perhaps the reason your baby is crying is she wants you to hold her. Babies are very attached to their mothers. They can even recognize their scent. If after you hold her she stops crying, try to cuddle her or put her to sleep.

Your baby may be sick. If your baby cries for hours and doesn't stop, especially after feeding her, you may want to see a doctor. Perhaps she is having problems with her tummy.

Sleep Little Baby

Teething. If your baby is between 4-7 months old, you may want to check her gums. At this age, babies usually get teeth already and it's painful.

Your baby just feels like crying. This is very normal. There are babies who cry for no reason at all. If your baby cries persistently for at least three hours, she may have colic. This crying condition is normal for a healthy baby. This usually occurs when your baby is about 2 weeks old, but it goes away after four months.

How to find out what he's crying about

For a first-time mom, it might be a little difficult to find out why your baby is crying. As you spend more time with your little one, you tend to recognize patterns and certain behaviors that allow you to determine the reason why your baby is crying. You could also check this list.

You may have noticed that newborns have a very high-pitched voice. This doesn't always mean that your baby is in pain. That's just how babies cry.

You will notice a baby is hungry when he fusses and squirms. When this happens, feed your baby right away.

If your baby is in pain, you will have a hard time consoling him. You will also see it in your baby's face that he's in pain.

How to Soothe a Crying baby

Consoling a crying baby is one of the most challenging jobs of a parent, but we are offering some of the gentle ways to soothe your crying baby. The first thing you should do when your baby starts crying is take a long deep breath and go with the basics. Feed your baby and change her diapers. Sometimes this will do the trick. If this doesn't work, just stay calm and try these tips:

Rock-a bye baby. Gently hold your baby in your arms and swivel back and forth. This often works but try not to overdo it. When you keep doing this every single time your baby cries, she becomes dependent.

Sleep Little Baby

Go with a soothing sound. Sometimes noises make a baby cry. Experiment with different background music and see which will work for your baby. You may want to sing to her as well. Sometimes she responds more to that.

Get your baby outside. They like looking at things especially colorful things. A change of scenery may calm and stop her from crying.

Get a swing for your baby. Movements help calm the baby. Create one specifically designed for your infant or toddler. Again, don't overdo this else your baby becomes dependent on the swing. She might not be able to fall asleep without it.

Try the 5 S's. The 5S are Swinging, Swaddling, Sucking, Side soothing, and using Sshhing sounds. Wrap your baby in a blanket or hold him on his side. You may also want to give your baby a pacifier.

Give your baby a soothing massage.

Check if the temperature inside your house is either too warm or too cold for the baby.

You may also want to check your baby's clothes. Perhaps they are too tight and she needs to change it. Always use loose clothes for your baby. They sleep better with those.

Talk to her gently. A baby listens to the mother. One of the most effective ways to soothe a baby is to talk to her quietly. Assure her that you will always be there for her.

Distract your baby with a toy.

Carry your baby. That makes her feel safe and secure.

Sometimes bathing can do wonders for the baby. Try giving your baby a warm bath before bedtime.

Try all the strategies mentioned above and see which one works for your baby and keep doing it.

Sleep Little Baby

How to Soothe a Crying Toddler

Do not tolerate negative behavior. It is best to start disciplining your child early. If your baby demands something you cannot give and he starts to cry, do not give in. Try not to let your anger set in as well. Be gentle with your child and refuse.

Give him something to do. A toddler likes to play during the day. Take him to a playgroup or any trips where there are other kids. This will surely make him tear-free.

There are times when you need to give in. If your toddler wants something, reconsider. Do not say no right away. If it doesn't harm him or your budget, say yes. That will surely stop his tears.

Gentle Ways to Put your Baby to Sleep

You may have tried all the ways of putting your baby to sleep, and they don't seem to work. Everyday, you keep losing sleep because your baby is awake when it's time for you to sleep. If you are a first-time mom, you may want to recognize sleeping signs from your baby first so you would know if he is ready to sleep or not. You need to spot signs if your baby is already tired. Look for these signs from your baby:

The baby rubs his eyes and tries to cry

The baby suddenly loses in interest in whatever he's doing. When he's playing with his toys, he throws it away

If you're carrying him, he may suddenly bury his face in your chest.

The baby suddenly becomes quiet

These signs are telling you that it's time to put the baby to sleep. Put him down on his cot and let him take his nap. As much as possible, avoid eye contact with your baby when you're trying to put him to sleep. That would only encourage the baby to snap out of him sleep zone.

When you see any of these signs, quietly put your baby to bed.

Sleep Little Baby

How to teach your baby to sleep soundly?

Babies do not yet know how sleeping works. As a parent, it is essential for you to teach your baby or toddler how and when to sleep. Following a routine is very helpful. As soon as your baby wakes up in the morning, open the curtains to allow sunlight to set into your home. This would let the baby know that it is time to wake up.

Do this every morning until the baby gets used to it. You may want to have background music on, something lively like nursery rhymes. When you have bathed and fed him, play with your baby. You should only play with your baby during the day.

At night, dim all lights and put some soothing music on. Prepare your baby for bed about two hours before bedtime. You may read him a book. Do not expose your baby to bright lights so he would know the difference between day and night.

If the baby tries to cry after putting him down, just pat the baby gently. Tell him it's okay because you're around. You may lie down together and cuddle her. Try to pretend you're also asleep so he knows it's really time to go to bed. Avoid carrying your baby while putting him to sleep. He becomes dependent on it over time.

You could also try these other tips:

Allow your baby to sleep on his own between six to eight months. This will make him not dependent on you all the time. When you see signs that the baby is already sleepy, gently put the baby to sleep. If she cries, pat her gently.

Try massaging your baby before sleeping. Before doing this, make sure the room is pleasant and comfortable to set the right mood. The massage should last not more than 15 minutes.

Give the baby a security object like a clean stuffed animal or a fresh baby blanket. For breastfeeding moms, try putting some breast milk on a piece of fabric and put it beside your baby. Since babies have strong sense of smell, the smell of the fabric may calm her.

Sleep Little Baby

Always attend to your baby's needs. If she wakes up crying in the night, find out why. Check her diapers as it might be full. Or your baby could be hungry.

Don't allow your baby to stay up too late. If he is still awake at 9pm, you might want to check his nap schedule. Schedule it in the early afternoon, not a couple of hours before bedtime.

When you feed him during the night, stay quiet. Avoid chatting with your baby so he knows it's time for bed.

Sleep problems and solutions for babies:

Problem: Your baby is awake at night and asleep during the day.

This means the baby still isn't aware that nighttime is for sleeping. To help your baby sleep, take her outside during the day. Socialize and play with her. Be active. You could take a walk in the park with your baby. Inside the house, allow plenty of sunlight to get in. Play some active music. Watch less television. At sundown, dim the lights and turn off television. Music should be soothing. Avoid a lot of talk with the baby to encourage him to sleep.

Problem: The baby wakes up in the middle of the night.

Do not turn on the lights when your baby wakes up. This shift might tell her brain it's time to wake up. What you can do is carry the baby for a few minutes then put the baby back in the bed. Wait for a few minutes until he is settled in, then leave the room quietly.

Ways to Put your Toddlers to Sleep

Toddlers need adequate sleep every night for their emotional and cognitive development. But they're very active and don't seem to want to go to sleep. When they're very tired and sleepy, they fight it. And they never get tired of playing. If you have a very challenging toddler, try these tips:

Help him set his biological clock. Set a time for sleeping every night. If possible, let him prepare for bed early, say about 7 pm. Avoid letting him sleep late or when he's very tired. When a toddler is

Sleep Little Baby

exhausted, his adrenalin and cortisol levels kick in. This would only keep him going. When this happens, toddlers find it harder to sleep during the night, and they wake up too soon. Dim the lights so he knows it's time to sleep. Avoid bright lights in his bedroom. Make him comfortable. His bed should be cozy. You may want to have a clean stuffed animal beside him to let him sleep right away.

Prepare a bedtime light snack for your toddler. Some toddlers prefer to eat before sleeping. While reading him stories, let him have a healthy snack and try something without sugar.

Get him sunlight and fresh air during the day. Let them play and socialize with other kids. Toddlers tend to sleep soundly during the night when they are active during the day. Just don't let them play a few hours before bedtime. It might just re-energize them. If you're good with humor, make your toddlers laugh. It's good for them.

Acknowledge your toddler's courage if he tries to sleep on his own. Talk to your toddler about sleeping alone and give him prizes in the morning if he doesn't cry or looks for you in his bed. Practicing motivation is good for the toddler. You can give him perhaps a new toy when you go out or food in the morning. Something he really likes to eat.

If a toddler is afraid to sleep in the dark, try telling him cheerful stories before bedtime. If he wakes up from a scary dream assure him it's gone now and that you're always there for him. Never tell him it's not real as dreams may seem very real to them. Just tell your toddler there is no need to worry.

Sleep problems and solutions for toddlers

Problem: Your toddler keeps getting in and out of bed.

If your toddler is already on his bed, but he keeps getting out, the reason is he doesn't want to go to sleep yet. You might want to try to do something creative with him. Try reading or listening to some relaxing music. You could also talk to him about a story you've read. If this doesn't work out, ask him what he needs. If he wants to get out of bed, let him. It's okay to sometimes make the child feels he is in control so long as you don't do it often.

Sleep Little Baby

Problem: Your child is already in bed for hours and he still can't sleep.

The one reason children can't sleep right away is because they have been playing or taking naps perhaps 1 or 2 hours before bedtime. Make sure naps are in the morning or early afternoon. Also, do not let your child play when it's almost bedtime.

Developing good sleeping practices with your baby or child

Sleeping is important to everyone's well-being and growth. For children, it makes them feel refreshed and alive during the day. They are unlikely to be irritable if they have a good night's sleep. Children remain alert and sharp when they are well rested. To help your child develop good sleeping habits, try these tips.

Try to minimize bedtime rituals. You may not completely eliminate this but being with your baby every time he is about to go to bed would make him dependent on you. You can still nurse or sing to him at bedtime but make sure you place him in his bed when he is still awake. It is better if he gets used to his mattress so in case he wakes up, he will not look for you.

Don't let your baby fall asleep with his bottle. If he gets used to it, he will depend on it as well. He will not be able to sleep without the bottle. The extra calories may also interfere with his body rhythms and might wake him up when his hungry or milk might pool on the baby's ear and will cause an infection. To avoid these, make sure you won't let him accustomed to have his bottle before bedtime.

Don't sleep with your baby beside you. Helping your baby sleep on his own would make him become independent. It would also reduce anxiety. If he's already used to it, try to eliminate it slowly until he gets used to sleeping alone.

Help him overcome his fear of being separated from you. At six months, your baby might feel abandoned if you're not with him when he sleeps. To avoid this, try to spend time with your baby about 15 minutes before he goes to bed. When he's already in his crib, talk for about five minutes and gently touch him. Then leave the room quietly.

Dealing with sleep problems

Bed-wetting

This is normal for younger children. This becomes a problem when the child is more than five years old and he still wets his bed at least twice a week. The best thing to do is let your child know it is a normal condition and that it is a no big deal.

You should also tell the other family members to not tease your child if he wet his bed. To help eliminate this problem, you need to monitor your toddler's fluid intake. You could also try waking him up after a few hours. If this doesn't help, try to talk to your pediatrician. He might be able to give you other options to help your child overcome this problem.

Sleep Deprivation

When your child isn't getting enough sleep, he will have trouble concentrating. He may perform poorly in school too. There are things you can do to find out if your child isn't getting enough sleep.

Observe if your child falls asleep when inside the car.

He doesn't wake up early in the morning.

You will notice that your child is overly sensitive and very irritable.

He sleeps way early than his usual bedtime.

If you see these signs, try to adjust his routines for him to have quality sleep every night.

Colic and How to Remedy it

One of the challenges of being a parent is when a baby cries for hours for no reason. Colic is a condition where babies less than 4 months old cries for about 3 hours a day and 3 days a week. This

Sleep Little Baby

happens to healthy babies, and it can be really stressful for a parent, but don't worry as it goes away after 3 or 4 months.

The cause of this condition is unknown. There was research done about colic, but they still couldn't figure out why it happens to healthy babies. Some of its symptoms include:

Crying episodes happen the same day every day for a few minutes to up to three hours. What a parent should do when this happens: Check your baby after crying as he might pass gas after a colic episode.

Intense crying. Colic is mysterious. No one really knows why it happens. When your baby cries, he is inconsolable. Nothing will make him stop crying.

Crying for no reason. When your baby has colic, he cries for no reason at all and you might notice some changes in the baby. He might clench his fists during a colic episode.

Some babies do not have Colic. Mothers who smoke before and after pregnancy contributes to an infant's colic.

Breastfed infants and first-borns are also not prone to colic. Colic disappears after 3 or 4 months. If it doesn't and you've tried doing everything to soothe your baby, talk to your pediatrician.

Here's what you can do before you make that appointment: Track how many times your baby cries and how many minutes or hours. Then write down how you've tried soothing your baby. You may list down other questions you have for the pediatrician.

Tips for soothing your baby:

Hold your baby gently during a colic episode. Hold them upright to prevent them to swallow air.

Have your baby burp after feeding.

Bath and massage your baby. This is very helpful and may calm the baby.

Chapter 5: Minimize Sleep Disruptors

Quite often, what deprives children of quality sleep aren't the conditions present during sleeping time but what they do shortly before it. In particular, the food and drinks children eat and drink, respectively, as well as children's activities shortly before bedtime can result in shallow and easily disrupted sleep. These include:

Food Intake: Do not feed your child food and drinks that are chock full of sugar because it'll make the child hyperactive just before bedtime, which will definitely make it hard for a child to sleep.

Extra-Curricular: Don't play with your child or do other activities with him – such as watching TV or playing video games on the tablet or on your smartphone – that are stimulating because it will make your child too stimulated to fall asleep early.

Errands: Avoid working your child's sleeping time around the errands you need to do or your other family activities. Do the opposite instead – work these activities around your child's sleep time. This will allow your toddler to get much needed quality snooze time on a regular basis.

Lighting: Use soft lights in the toddler's room at night as the child winds down to sleep because bright lights hinder the production of the sleep hormone melatonin, which will make it harder to fall asleep at night. When the child is about to sleep, turn off the lights or if he/she is uncomfortable in total darkness, keep a small lamp on that will give enough soft light to appease your child enough to be able to go to sleep. This will help keep the room just dark enough to be conducive to sleeping.

Sleeping Cues

It will be too late if you only put your child to sleep when he's already acting tired. The best time to put him to bed is when he starts exhibiting sleeping cues and not when already exhausted. What do these cues look like?

In general, they include him being cranky, unable to focus his attention on anything, yawning and eye-rubbing. Observe your child carefully to discover what his unique sleeping cues are so that you won't miss them when they happen. Failure to catch those cues and act accordingly can make it much harder for him to go to sleep as, by then, he will already be frantic, jumpy, or wired.

The Importance of Consistency

To help your child sleep well easily at night, you need to make the child feel a sense of inevitability, safety and calmness. And these can be accomplished by establishing a regular routine that may involve taking a nice warm bath, bedtime story reading, kissing, prayers or blessings and bed tucking right before turning off the lights for sleep. With bedtime routines, it's important not to overdo them. Doing so may take up excess time and make your child miss his sleeping windows of opportunity and have a hard time sleeping afterward.

What if your child becomes resistant or stubborn with the routine and chooses not to go with the flow? Just try to make the clock the bad guy, instead of you! How? One way to do this is by making your child a simple chart of the steps involved in the bedtime routine, which you can post in this child's room. Each step on the chart should feature a picture of your child doing each step and a clock's time that corresponds to the time at which each of the activities must be accomplished. As you go through the bedtime routine you want to establish every night with your child, point to the relevant photos. In time, your child will gradually want to cooperate.

An even better way to do this is by giving him an incentive. You can say something like:

"Hey, it's 7:00 already! You know what? We can have an extra story to read later, just before lights out, if you finish brushing your teeth now."

That should give your child the opportunity to see you as his ally rather than a stern drill sergeant. More than that, it allows him to

Sleep Little Baby

develop a good sense of personal responsibility and the ability to make wise choices later on.

Wind Down Early

Don't expect an easy time putting your child to bed if you abruptly stop his activities and expect him to go cold turkey! Your child needs enough time to wind down, relax and be in the mood to hit the sack. To allow for this, give your child an hour or two of quiet and calmness in order to slowly wind down into a relaxed state of mind and body that's conducive to deep and restful sleep throughout the night.

A Comfortable Sleeping Environment

As part of their normal sleep cycles, it's normal for toddlers to wake up slightly in the middle of their sleep. They usually return to a deep state of slumber relatively quickly. As a parent, what you must concern yourself with is that they don't fully wake up during those "semi" wake up moments in the middle of the night due to a feeling or sense of discomfort. To ensure this doesn't happen, it will be worth investing in a bed or mattress that makes your child sleep comfortably through those minor sleep-waking moments.

Another factor that determines how comfortable your child's sleeping environment can be is room temperature. A room that's too hot or too cold can make it uncomfortable enough to disrupt your child's sleep. During the summer months, a breezy or air-conditioned room can help your child sleep comfortably while a warm pair of PJs and nice warm blanket can make it comfortable for him to sleep during the icy months of the year.

Another factor that influences your child's ability to sleep comfortably is lighting – or lack of it. Light makes people feel awake and makes it hard for them to sleep so it's best to use soft lights in your child's room especially during the last hour or two before sleeping, as I mentioned earlier. It will also help if you make his room as dark as is comfortably possible when he's already sleeping. Light makes it hard for your child's body to produce melatonin, which is a key sleeping hormone. So keep the lights down…or off.

The Biological Clock

If you want your toddler to sleep well, his body must learn how to anticipate or expect sleep at a specific time in the evening. For most toddlers, going to sleep between 6:30 p.m. and 8:00 p.m. is the ideal.

While it may be tempting to think that sleeping later in the evening will tire your child out and make him fall asleep more easily, it won't. When he stays up late, stress hormones such as cortisol and adrenalin start kicking in due to being over-tired, which will make him do as the Energizer bunny does… keep going and going and going and going. By then, it'll be much harder for him to sleep at night. After that, you'll have a hard time sleeping due to the stress.

And when he has a hard time falling asleep, guess what? He'll wake up more frequently throughout the night and will tend to wake up earlier in the day. When that happens, expect a cranky toddler during the day. Just continue experimenting with different sleeping times until you're able to see which time is optimal in terms of minimizing or keeping your child from being all wound up.

Another way to establish a consistent sleeping routine is turning by down the lights at least one hour prior to going to bed. Coupled with calm and slow routines, it helps program your child's body and mind to anticipate falling asleep at a certain time in the evening. A consistent, slow and calm pre-sleeping routine is a very effective way to lull your child to sleep compared to one that's abrupt, such as simply putting him in pajamas and turning off the lights within 2 minutes.

The key sleeping cue to watch out for here (remember our discussion on sleeping cues?) is him starting to becoming sleepy. Once you continue letting him stay awake past this moment, his body will switch to overdrive and stimulate him with adrenaline to the point when it will be very hard, if not downright impossible, to lull him into a deep and restful sleep soon.

Don't Deny the Naps Too Soon

Most toddlers are neither emotionally nor physiologically prepared to give up their regular naps – at least not until they turn 3 years old. Thus, you might consider taking it easy on your child if he still wants to take naps throughout the day before the age of 3. If you deny the toddler that, both of you will pay a heftier price in the evening – and the following day – when your child becomes too adrenalized and cranky to sleep early.

Midnight Snacks

Particularly during those growth spurt years, toddlers need to eat midway into the night. Some of the best choices for midnight snacks that won't disrupt their sleep are calming and predictable food and drinks such as a piece of toast, a slice of turkey and a glass of warm milk. The key is to choose food and drinks that are neither stimulating nor loaded with sugar. You can move your child much better through your pre-sleep routine if you can make the child eat a snack at a table in the child's room as you read them their bedtime stories. Just make sure he brushes his teeth afterward, just before going to sleep.

If your toddler still tends to still fall asleep with a feeding bottle in hand and mouth, you should disassociate him from it. Doing so will enable him to easily go back to sleep during those slight waking moments in the middle of the night because he won't be stimulated into waking up completely as he drinks from the bottle.

Regular Exercise, Laughter, and the Great Outdoors

It turns out the old folks are right when they say that for kids to sleep more soundly at night, they need to play outdoors as much as possible and not just sit inside the house playing computer games or watching TV all the time. This is great for your child too for as long as it's not a few hours before bedtime, as it will just make your toddler too energized in the evening to the point of having a difficult time sleeping.

It's also important that your child gets to laugh often because doing so allows him to bring down his stress hormone levels. Kids who normally have a hard time falling and staying asleep at night are those that carry a lot of emotional baggage. Laughing heartily and frequently can help your toddler unload emotional baggage (if he has any) to fall deeply asleep at night.

Develop New Habits for Sleeping

You may be doing your child a disservice if you're always rocking or nursing him to sleep. Why? You're making him get used to always being with you while asleep. This may result in him always looking for you as his security blanket in order to be able to go back to sleep during those mini waking times throughout the night. And that's part of his normal sleep cycle. When you're not there, going back to sleep will be very hard or practically impossible.

Your child's pre-sleep routine may not necessarily involve rocking or nursing the toddler to sleep but may nevertheless make it hard for him to go back to sleep on his own when he wakes up slightly in the middle of the night. Thus, it's important that you help him develop new sleeping habits that will empower him to sleep soundly on his own.

It may be hard at first so it's best to do this one step at a time. For example, instead of going cold turkey and just stopping rocking him to sleep, you can start by rocking him for shorter periods of time until you completely stop doing so. It'll be very difficult to develop new sleeping habits by simply going cold turkey on the one you want to replace. It must be done, pardon the pun, in baby steps.

Don't Rush It

Speaking of establishing new and independent sleeping habits, start by holding him while he goes off to sleep but not in a lying position because that puts you at risk of falling asleep as well! To help you to relax and make the most of this bonding moment, just meditate or listen to soft music.

Once your child is accustomed to falling asleep as you hold him, you should start making him accustomed to falling asleep by simply holding his hand or placing your hand on his head or forehead. You can also choose to substitute this by using a big stuffed toy or pillow in your place. Kids often love cuddling and curling around a nice, soft stuffed animal or a pillow, although it is important to choose a toy that is safe.

When your child is already able to fall asleep simply by being touched and not held, try sitting beside your child while he falls asleep. At first, you'll need to sit really close so that your child can touch you easily when he reaches out to you.

The last frontier is when your child's able to fall asleep without any physical contact with you. You then start to move your seat slowly further and further away from your child until you're able to exit the room. In moments that your child wakes up and tries to sit up, just say, "Lie down now please…it's sleep time, it's bed time." in a monotone voice.

You can also try and do something around the room while your child falls asleep. Just make sure what you'll be doing isn't noisy or will in any way distract your child from his sleep. Doing this will give your sleeping child a sense of security with your presence in the room and your proximity. You can then begin staying outside your child's room for longer and longer periods of time until you're able to finally help your child develop the habit of sleeping independently.

On those days that your child backslides and needs your physical touch again, don't sweat it. It won't derail the overall progress for as long as it doesn't happen frequently and consecutively. Just keep at it and the independent sleeping habit will eventually be established.

Lying Down with the Child on the Adult Bed

It's easy for most toddlers, yours included probably, when parents lie down with them on their beds. This can be especially challenging for the parents because often times, they themselves fall asleep and would have to wake up just to go their own rooms, at which point their sleep's already disrupted. Their evening sleep's practically ruined by then. It also makes the child dependent on the presence of the parents to fall and stay asleep, which is a behavior that actually needs to be corrected.

That's why some parents choose to let their toddler or baby sleep in their own bed until they're old enough to sleep on their own. It minimizes the disruption in their sleep. And most kids are able to adjust well to sleeping in their own beds and rooms as they reach a certain age so this strategy is one that many parents have adopted.

There's no right or wrong between the two. As the parent of your toddler, you're in the best position to see which option is best for your child, especially when it comes to helping him get deep and restful sleep.

Let Your Child Know What Will Happen

For this, you can do something fun. Pretend to act out a mini-play using props such as your child's stuffed toys and if none are available, use his pillows. Here, one of the "characters" will play the part of putting off bedtime. Using the props, act out what will actually happen as part of the pre-sleep routine.

For example, you act out the part of the "parents" by saying "It's bed time!" Then, you can act out the baby's role (represented by one of the props) asking to be cuddled or rocked to sleep in reaction to the call to go to bed. Next, you also act out the parents' response to the request where they say "No, we will just hold you as you go to bed." Then, you can act out the part where the baby prop cries, to which the parents respond by holding the child until he eventually settles down and sleeps.

When acting out the firmness part of the skit, it's important to do so in a calm and loving manner that firmly insists that the child should already sleep. Over time, your child can identify with the "baby" prop and sees that it eventually goes to sleep. The key here is to show through your skit that the parents always assure the child that they will always be there for him.

Chapter 6: How To Use Simple Steps To Help Your Kids Sleep In 48 Hours

The rule of these steps

What comes to your mind when someone mentions the Cry it out (CIO) method to you? I'm pretty sure that your maternal instincts kick in and that makes you all judgmental about the person mentioning it. Cry it out method is a practice that is highly misunderstood by most of the people out there until they take out time to sit down and read about it. No, it isn't a single technique that tells you to leave your little one to cry in his/her crib alone until he/she gets tired enough to fall back to sleep. If this is what you're against then I'm with you as it is definitely a cruel way to force a baby to sleep but again, this isn't what CIO is.

There is more than one reason why a child may be fussy when you're helping them learn to self-soothe. You should learn the difference between if the child is crying to get your attention or if he/she really is inconvenienced and in need of your assistance.

It takes time for a baby to learn a new skill: self-soothing. We as adults can get quite fussy when it comes to change. So how can you blame a baby? Just as adults get over their temporary stress with time as they adjust, so do babies. When they are put in the crib to sleep, they may cry because they are stressed about the change. This temporary stress won't damage the baby's mental health. Instead, learning how to self-soothe will develop grit and problem-solving skills in him/her.

CIO is a technique that is a part of other methods to help you train your child to fall sleep himself/herself.

1-6 months

It is crucial to set a routine for babies as early as possible. The method that really worked for Ella and Shaun was a 3-hour cycle. I started it when they were 1 weeks old. It includes three activities:

Sleep Little Baby

feeding, playing and sleeping. For instance, if Ella woke up at 6 am, I would feed her at 6 am, play with her for 30 minutes and put her back to sleep around 8 am. The next feed would be at 9 am, 12 pm, 3 pm, 6 pm, 9 pm and the last feeding time would be 12 pm. In the first month, you may need to feed one more time at 3 am. Once you notice the baby doesn't wake up at 3 am, you can skip it. For Ella and Shaun, I was able to stop night feeding when they were 1 month old. The routing slightly changed when both were 3-6 months. The 3-hours circle extended to 4-hours, which means that if they woke up at 6 am, their first feed would be at 6 am, 10 am, 2 pm, 6 pm and the last feeding time would be 10 pm. All the activities will be the same: feed, play and sleep. The only difference is that you should extend playing time with the baby since his/her waking hours are longer.

In the last feed, you need to skip the playtime and put your baby to sleep right after feeding and burping. If the baby wakes up in the middle of the night or wakes up too early for no reason (poop or sickness etc.), ignore him/her so that they go back to sleep. Most of the babies should get used to the routine within 48 hours.

There was a very big difference in my experiences of sleep training Ella and Shawn. When I analyzed it, other than the differences in resistance techniques of my two little masterminds, the way I reacted to their journey of settling in the new habit played a very important role. Naturally, for Ella's sleep training, I was a new mommy and that added more stress for me. I checked up on her a few times a night in the beginning, at times this would wake her up and ultimately it used to result in both of us being unrested the following day.

After I adopted the CIO method introduced by our pediatrician, I was pretty impressed with how well the technique worked on the first night. I realized that when Ella cried a couple of times through the night, most of the times she would slip back to sleep in less than 10 minutes. I would wait for 20 minutes after the sound stopped and entered her room to check her condition. From day 2, she was sleeping soundly through the night and so was I. Because of this experience, when it is much easier to train Shaun. He was also able

Sleep Little Baby

to sleep through a night on the second night, once I start his sleep training.

The steps above to set up routine for the baby were proven very effective not just for me but for many friends with whom I shared the technique with. Sleeping through the night is extremely beneficial for the mom and the baby. Moms, you need your energy to recharge so that you can report back to mommy duties attentively the next morning and feel confident of yourself.

There are a number of external factors that contribute to the success/failure of the CIO. Room temperature is one of these factors. The temperature of the room should neither be too hot nor too cold. Light is another factor. During the morning napping, I normally closed the curtain to make sure that the baby can sleep in the darker room.

Another thing to take into account is making sure that at this stage your baby does not get used to sleeping in your arms or falling asleep when being rocked because it will create problems for you later when the baby starts to depend on it. Similarly, make sure that the baby does not sleep while being fed either.

Example for the 3-hour cycle:

6 AM	9 AM	12 PM			
Feed	Play & Sleep	Feed	Play & Sleep	Feed	Play & Sleep

3 PM	6 PM	9 PM			
Feed	Play & Sleep	Feed	Play & Sleep	Feed	Play & Sleep

12 AM	3 AM	6 AM
Last Feed	Sleep Optional	Feed

6-12 months

Sleep Little Baby

In this stage, the method will stay the same as above. Your baby should already be habituated to a routine. One of the differences is a longer wake up time (4-5 hours), so you would need to adjust the time for each circle, from 4 hours to 4.5-5 hours for example. The other major difference is that the baby starts to have mashed food, so their food intake is much more. If your baby wakes up at 6 am, the first feed could be 6 am, 10.30 am, 3 pm, and 7.30 pm. You can skip the feed at 12 am if your baby can sleep over.

Example for the 4.5-hour cycle:

6 AM	**10:30 AM**	**3 pm**
Feed Play & Sleep	Feed Play & Sleep	Feed Play & Sleep

7:30 PM	**12 AM**	**6 AM**
Feed Play & Sleep	Optional	Sleep Feed

Toddler

Again, the principle of the method will be similar to the previous ones. The biggest challenge would be that your little one will shift to a bed from the crib, which will give him/her the freedom to walk out and come to you after you have put him/her to bed. You will find yourself to be facing a completely different ball game.

When Ella moved to the bed, she'd always jump out after we put her sleep, followed us to our room and asked us to stay with her in the room. I was completely clueless about how to deal with this new situation. It is different from the previous model: the baby was confined to the crib and you can put them down and leave. I was back to square one, staying 1 hour or more to accompany and pat her. Most of the time, she was guarded. The moment I removed my hand from her body, she would wake up and cry. The worst part is that she would wake up a couple of times in the middle of the night and run to our room. It was a big battle to put her back to sleep. None of us could have a healthy and consistent sleep, which resulted in everyone being frustrated and upset.

Luckily, we got the advice from one of our close friends, Dina, who is also a baby sleeping consultant. She explained to us what we did was actually preventing Ella from self-soothing. Because Ella was expecting we would leave, naturally, she was guarded and couldn't have sound sleep. Children's brain hasn't developed proper logic thinking, so as parents, we need to send a direct message to help them have the right behavior. We need to let her know if she doesn't sleep in the night time, no one is going to play with her. Dina asked us to reestablish the bedtime routine to make sure it suits Ella's development and told us how to act after we put her to sleep.

Here is the example that we reset Ella's sleeping schedule:

7 am   1 pm   2 pm   9 pm   9:30 pm

Wake up   Nap Time   Wake up from Nap   Start   the Bedtime Routine   Turn on night light & walk out from the room.

Important things when you reset the schedule:

•   Don't let him/her take a long nap that exceeds 2 hours as it will make it harder for your child to go to sleep at night.

•   The afternoon nap and the bedtime should be at least 7-8 hours apart.

•   For the 1st sleep training night, you can even prolong the bedtime to 10 or 10.30 pm so you can leverage your kid's fatigue. Make sure that your child has some physical activities after nap so he/she is tired.

After you reestablish the sleep schedule, you would need to build nighttime routine to let your children understand it is a bedtime.

There are several things that you can do to prepare your child's mind for bed. A repeated nighttime routine will let your child wind down

Sleep Little Baby

and give him/her hint that it is a bedtime. Here are some tips you should consider when you set up nighttime routine:

- Start the routine 20 to 30 minutes before bedtime.
- Try to keep the activities subtle so that the kid can calm down before bedtime.
- Reading bedtime stories is highly recommended. Both of my kids always look forward to choosing the storybooks and enjoy intimacy with us before bedtime.

After tucking the baby in and kissing him/her good night, you need to leave the room immediately. The trick to stop them from coming to your room is to lock yourself in your room. Don't lock their room or confine them in their room. By doing this, you are sending a direct message to your kid: it is sleeping time, and no one will play with you.

Ignore the fuss he/she makes outside of your door. No attention from you will make them go back to their bed and sleep eventually. Most of the children will change their behavior and adopt the new routine within 48 hours.

The first day of training will be toughest for most of parents. Though Dina warned us about the duration of the cry we may experience, it was still much harder to handle it.

After I put Ella to bed on that night, I told her I won't stay in her room to pat her to sleep and she needs to stay in the bed. Ella didn't realize the game was changing until I left and stayed in my room. She started to run to our door and stayed there crying.

During the hour she was crying outside the door, Jack and I needed to hold each other's hand not to open the door. Since we were exhausted and lacking in proper sleep for months, we desperately wanted the technique to work. We were expecting Ella would even sleep outside our door, but she went to back to her bed and slept after an hour of crying.

On the 2nd night, we were expecting the same pattern to repeat but a miracle happened. When she ran to our door and saw the door was closed, she ran back to her room immediately and cried for 10 minutes before drifting to sleep. Jack and I looked at each other and couldn't believe that it actually worked on the 2nd night as what Dina mentioned.

After the 2nd night, Ella repeated the same pattern 2-3 times for the next 2 weeks, but she always went back to her bed and slept quickly.

Things to consider

To implement this, there are a few things that parents need to take into account while instilling healthy sleeping habits in toddlers. I will address them in this section.

1. The sense of safety:

Firstly, you must ensure that when you do sleep training, the child's sleeping environment stays consistent and safe. Since you will leave his/her room door open, make sure the living area is tidy for him/her to wander and also keep a small lamp or the toilet light on to prevent him/her from tripping. To be on the safe side, consider baby-proofing the apartment.

2. Offering Minimum Soothing

Knowing when to step in to soothe the child yourself is important. Generally, kids don't cry over 30-40 minutes (except 1st night). If your child is crying over that time, check on him/her and offer some water. If your kid is not ill and just fussing around to get your attention, you should give him minimum soothing and walk out.

If the child abruptly stops crying, don't walk into the room as soon as it happens because the child is often in the phase of drifting back to sleep. It is best to wait 20-30 minutes before checking up on him/her. If you go in right away, the crying and fussing around will start again.

3. Stick to the routine:

Sticking to the routine, no matter what is essential. This means, even if the previous night, your baby didn't go to sleep on time or any event happened that disrupted the routine, don't let it ruin the next day's routine. Wake the child up on time and don't extend the napping time. The child may be fussy for the day but in the long-term, this will benefit the whole family.

Questions when you adopt this approach

Q: Should I still wake the baby up at 7 am if she remained awake a lot during the night?

The answer to this is yes, you should. Letting the child sleep will make him more active and push down the napping time, which will further push down the bedtime and ultimately ruin the bedtime routine that you worked so hard to establish. Your child might be a little fussier than usual during the day but trust me, starting from the next day; everything will go back to normal.

Q: What if the baby wakes up at 4:30 am or 5 am?

If the child wakes up in the middle of the night, you must ignore him/her and let him/her go back to sleep.

Q: It's been 3-4 days, but the child is still crying. Why isn't it getting better?

If it's been 3-4 days and the process isn't working, this means that you're doing something wrong. Though it is normal, working within 48 hours for most of the cases, you should expect kids will test you on the 4th or 5th day. Eventually, he/she should be going to bed within 15-20 minutes.

The common mistake that parents make is that they put the child in a bed after they fall asleep. The key is to tuck them in when they are drowsy but not asleep. This is to ensure that the child is learning to fall asleep him/herself. Getting this step right is crucial otherwise the whole process will fail for a number of reasons. One of them is that the child is not learning to fall asleep by himself/herself. The other is that when they wake up in the middle of the night and cannot find you beside themselves, they will panic, which will result in the adrenaline rush and the traces of sleep will disappear.

The other common mistake is inappropriate sleep timings. If your baby is taking long naps or you're not waking them up on time in the morning, they won't experience fatigue at night, which will keep them up. Make sure that there are 7-8 hours between afternoon nap and bedtime.

If you did all of the above properly, the baby is still crying after day 4 and 5, you should check with your pediatrician or sleeping consultant to identify if there is some other problem.

Q: After we come back from holiday or after someone visits us, how can we get back to the sleep routine?

Kids would have some free pass while holidaying or when someone visits and stays with us. It is always very difficult to bring the kids back to the routine. The trick is that you need to be back to sleep training immediately after a holiday or any break, so they can see the difference and get back to the sleeping routine quickly.

Q: Will this method affect kids' mental development?

Kids' resilience is greater than you think. Such short-term stress is different from the long-term one. Instead of affecting their mental development, this method can help them learn how to couple with the stress and behave properly. As long as you do this with love, the kids would receive the message.

Chapter 7: Importance Of Establishing A Good Bedtime Routine

Whether you're using a self-soothing method or another no-tears technique, parents must understand the importance of developing a bedtime routine first. It helps you win half the battle if you could somehow communicate with your baby what to expect next, and you get just that by having a consistent bedtime ritual. Babies really do appreciate the consistency and predictability of a good bedtime routine. They need to feel relaxed and be in an environment that tells them it's time to sleep. It is important to find a right bedtime routine for your baby as early as you possibly can. Aim to have a pattern established by the time your baby is about 8 weeks old.

For a sleep routine to be successful, you need to ensure that it is short and simple. Once again, a 20-minute routine will suffice, and it could be as simple as first a warm bath and then diaper and jammies followed by a story in the rocking chair. However, the fact is that different babies have different sleep needs, so you have to find a combination of what seems best for your baby.

The Feeding Schedule

With newborns, it's all about calories and getting their tummies full. Newborns need a set amount of calories a day. We can eat three meals a day and get all the calories we need to sustain us throughout the night without us waking up hungry at some point during the night.

Infants, on the other hand, need to eat throughout the night because they haven't reached enough calories and need to eat more. One of the reasons they have to eat so often is because their stomachs are so tiny at this point in development. If their stomachs were larger, they wouldn't need to eat as often because they would be able eat more in one sitting like us. As your baby gets older, s/he will eat more and it will sustain them for longer periods of time.

Sleep Little Baby

When you first bring your baby home, you'll find that your baby probably wants to eat every two to three hours, both morning and at night. Most pediatricians will recommend that you let your baby dictate when s/he wants to eat for the first few weeks.

After the first few weeks, however, you can start to implement more of a regulated feeding schedule. If you really want your baby to sleep through the night, feed your baby more often during the day. In this manner, s/he will not need to eat as often during the night. Even if your baby isn't crying or signaling to you that they want to eat, feed them anyway.

At first, they may not eat much, but eventually they will grow accustomed to the feeding schedule and will start to eat more and more at each feeding and less during the night. Below is a feeding schedule you can try out. According to this schedule, you would be feeding your baby every 2 ½ hours starting at 7:30 AM.

The feedings will be at:

7:30 AM, 10:00 AM, 12:30 PM, 3:00 PM, 5:30 PM, 8:00 PM, 10:30 PM, and so on.

Let your baby feed for as long as s/he wants if you are breastfeeding, and if you are bottle feeding, prepare plenty of formula. You will quickly learn how much s/he will drink each time. If your baby is napping during a scheduled feeding time, wake them up. You will be grateful later during the night when they sleep longer.

Some moms even shorten the time period to 2 hours; however, some babies struggle to eat that frequently. You can try both to determine what works best for you and your baby.

Feeding schedules are rigorous, and you will feel like you are feeding your baby constantly at first. And realistically, it doesn't leave you with much time to get other things done. For instance, if you need to go to the grocery store, you'll feed your baby and have to run quickly in order to make it back in time for their next feeding time. Eventually, as your baby grows older, you can stretch the times to three hours but only as their stomach grows bigger and they can handle more milk or formula.

Sleep Little Baby

By giving them as much milk or formula as they can eat throughout the day, you increase the likelihood of them staying asleep longer during the night without needing to eat. At first, they will probably still need at least one or two feedings during the night because their stomach is still so small, but compare that to waking every two or three hours to eat. You will get stretches of four hours or more after just a few days of implementing a strong feeding schedule.

Help Your Baby Get Rid of Pent-Up Energy

After some time has passed since they were fed and burped, your baby will sleep better at night if you help them get rid of any pent-up energy in their system. Different activities will help you achieve this task. You can help them dance a bit to the tune of a catchy song, let them bounce in their bouncer, or even give your little one a "horsey" ride. These types of activities will leave your baby feeling more relaxed before bedtime if they are followed by calmer and quieter activities such as giving them a bath or reading them a storybook.

Give Your Baby a Warm Bath

A bath will go a long way in making your baby feel relaxed, especially after a few hours of play. Let your baby sit in warm water for a soothing experience. Recent research conducted in the UK reveals that almost 60% of babies have a bath every night, with all of them spending an average of 15 minutes in the water. However, if you happen to notice signs indicating that your baby is irritated or even too excited during baths, you may be better off leaving this activity out of your bedtime ritual.

Wash Your Baby's Hands and Face

When a bath is out of the question, you can include washing in your routine. Start by washing your baby's face and hands. Afterwards, brush their teeth a bit — the earlier they get used to that, the better. Lastly, a diaper change may also give your baby a signal that it's time to sleep.

Give Your Baby Verbal Reassurance

Sleep Little Baby

You can simply have a quick chat with your little man or girl before you put them in their crib for sound, restful sleep. Talking to your baby will be a relaxing experience not only for your baby but for you as well.

Read a Bedtime Story

Get a storybook with colorful pictures. You can lay your baby in their crib and gently rock it from side to side while you read for a few minutes. It is a good idea to start this routine when your baby is as young as 8 weeks.

Say Goodnight to Their Favorite Toys

Walk around with your baby in your arms and say goodnight to his or her favorite toys or objects. It's an interesting activity to include in the bedtime routine, and many parents have found it quite effective because babies enjoy being carried.

Chapter 8: Sleep Solutions and Strategies

It is important to understand that no two babies are going to be the exact same. Even if the babies are siblings, they are likely going to have different sleep needs. What works to get one baby to sleep soundly will not work for another. There is some trial and error involved as you figure out what solutions and strategies work best for you and your baby. Do not be dismayed if your sister or best friend tells you this method worked like a dream for her, but your baby absolutely refuses to cooperate. Everybody has different ways of doing things and it is just going to take a little practice to figure out what your sleeping trick is going to be.

Please know that you cannot give up on a single solution after one night. Give it a week or so to give your child the chance to adapt to your new method. If it still isn't working, then it is probably a good time to tweak your habits or try something new altogether.

Preventing SIDS

Sleeping is important to a baby's health, but proper sleeping positions are crucial in the prevention against SIDs. Medical professionals recommend infants be put to sleep on their backs. Your parents or older babysitter will tell you this is wrong, but things have changed over the past 20 years. It has been revealed that the back is best when it comes to laying a baby in bed.

All those stuffed toys are cute and cuddly, but they should never be placed in the baby's crib, cradle or bassinet. Along with that, you don't want your baby's bed to be too soft. The mattress needs to be firm. Don't put too many blankets on your baby at night. Warm clothing and a single blanket are usually enough. When possible, sleep in the same room with your baby those first weeks and months. You will be in tune to your baby's breathing and will likely hear when he is in distress.

Lastly, don't smoke around your baby—ever. If at all possible, keep your baby away from all secondhand smoke. Some experts believe putting a baby to sleep with a pacifier is also helpful in preventing SIDs, but the correlation between the two hasn't been confirmed. Giving your baby a pacifier when he goes to bed can help the baby sleep better during the first 12 months.

Birth to 4 Months

It seems like you have waited forever to get that little bundle of joy in your arms, but now you are hoping to put the baby down for a little while so you can get some sleep. The first few months after the baby is born are an exciting time. You will likely have lots of visitors who want to see and hold the baby. All the activity can make it difficult for you and your baby to settle into a nice routine. It is tough to plan visits around a newborn's schedule. They need a lot of sleep and a constant stream of visitors can be difficult to manage.

The following sleep solutions can help you get your baby to sleep after a busy day of visiting:

Stop playing - Your newborn will only be awake for short periods of time before he starts to get sleepy. He may want to stay awake a bit longer so he can absorb his surroundings and most importantly, study you. When you notice your baby getting sleepy or it is time for a nap or bed, it is time to stop playing. Don't make direct eye contact with the little one as you rock him to sleep or feed him. Eye contact is stimulating to the baby and he will be eager to stay awake all night watching you.

Put baby down - When the baby has been awake for an hour or so or you can tell he is getting sleepy, put the baby in his bed and stay nearby. It is an excellent opportunity to teach the baby how to fall asleep on his own. It helps to have some white noise to help soothe the baby. It may be the radio, television or even the dishwasher running. When it is too quiet, the baby may struggle to fall asleep.

Infant swings - The gentle swaying of a swing is soothing to some babies—not all. Recline the seat, strap the baby in and put the swing on the low setting to gently rock the baby to sleep. This gives you a free moment as well as puts baby to sleep. You can try moving the baby to his bed after he has been lulled to sleep in the swing. This

Sleep Little Baby

takes some practice and you will have to learn whether or not your child appreciates the move after he has fallen asleep.

Crying it out - This is something that has lost a lot of favor with parents of today's generation. Infants cry for a particular reason, not because they want to. A whimper or a little fussing is considered okay to leave alone to let the child try and soothe himself back to sleep. However, a constant cry usually indicates the child is distressed and needs attention. When the baby fusses, stand near the bed and quietly talk to the baby to try and allay any troubles. Sometimes a comforting hand on the baby's abdomen is all that is needed to give the baby a little comfort knowing mom or dad is nearby.

Turn out the lights - Use room darkening shades, blinds or curtains to help block the light when it is naptime or when you want the baby to sleep past sunrise. You want to help train the child that darkness is associated with sleep. By setting the mood in the room, your baby will soon start picking up on the signal that it is time to slow down and sleep. A nightlight is perfectly fine and advisable. Be aware also of intrusions such as street lights and your neighbors motion activated garage lights that can split the darkness in your baby's room.

Old fashioned rocking - Rocking chairs have been used to rock babies to sleep for hundreds of years for a reason—they work! A nice slow rocking motion is very soothing. Let the baby snuggle close and he will likely fall asleep in no time. There are a couple of different approaches to putting the baby down. You will need to figure out what works best for your baby.

1-When the baby is quiet and content and on the verge of sleep, gently put him in bed.

Allow the baby to fall into a deep sleep on his own.

2-Wait until the baby is in a deep sleep before placing him on his back in bed.

Swaddling - Newborns have been living in a cramped area with their limbs wrapped tightly about them for months. When they are

Sleep Little Baby

introduced to the bright, loud world, it is only natural they would feel safer when wrapped up tight. Swaddling gives them that safety and comfort they need in order to relax enough to let sleep take them. The nurses in the hospital will typically show parents how to properly swaddle a baby. There are also plenty of blankets with Velcro that make it easy to swaddle the child. Before putting the baby to bed, swaddle the child.

4 Months to 1 Year

By this age, your baby is learning more about sleep habits and will be more prepared to accept routines. This is an excellent time for you to start establishing bedtime routines and established bedtimes.

Soothing bath - A soothing, warm bath is one way to signal to the baby that bedtime is imminent. The warm water helps relax the baby. You can use some lavender infused baby washes to take advantage of the calming effects of lavender. Keep play time to a minimum as you start setting the mood for sleep.

Rituals - Establish a ritual that suits your baby and you. If it is the warm bath, a fresh diaper, nursing/bottle and rocking for five minutes before laying the child in bed, go for it. Be consistent to teach the child what each of the steps indicates. When it is bath time, your baby will learn bedtime is imminent. He will start to settle and look forward to the feeding and cuddling before bed. Your ritual may be different. Do what works best for you!

Give a full belly - Babies of this age will not need to eat as often as newborns, but they will still need to eat every few hours. You can help your baby sleep longer by starting to fill the tummy an hour or two before bed. Instead of feeding every three hours, feed the baby two hours before bed and then again just before bedtime. This will hopefully earn you a longer block of sleep before the child is hungry again.

Slings or Mobys - About 30 minutes before it is time for the child to go down for a nap or bed, put the baby in a sling or Moby and go about your business. The gentle swaying of your movement, combined with the closeness and sound of your heart beating will help lull the child into sleep. It is also the signal to the child that it is no longer time to play.

Pacing - Walking around the living room with the baby snuggled up against your shoulder is an old trick. The movement is soothing to the baby. Singing or talking often helps soothe the child. The vibration in your chest as you talk to the baby or to others is comforting. Throw the baby's favorite blanket over him and rub the back while walking around the room. As the baby gets older, this can prove more difficult as the child gets heavier.

Gadgets - You have seen the plethora of Teddy Bears that "breathe," mobiles, crib toys and other gear that is all designed to create white noise to remind the child of being in the womb. It is supposed to be soothing and help lull the child into a deep sleep. The truth is these things only work with some babies. Some children are agitated by the constant noise. However, they do work and your baby just may be one of those who can fall asleep to the sounds produced by these gadgets. One recommendation—if it a singing, humming or talking gizmo, find one that allows you to record your voice for the child to fall asleep too just in case the toy is not always around.

1 year to 2 years

By a year of age, your child will be familiar with your bedtime habits. If you have a ritual in place, keep with it if it is working. It will likely need tweaking to accommodate your child's development. If you are still struggling to get your child to sleep and to stay asleep, try some of these techniques. It is never too late to implement a new ritual that is more effective.

Loosen up - Newborns appreciate swaddling, while babies and toddlers prefer to have room to move. Keep the blankets to a minimum. A single cotton blanket will likely be enough. You will know what works best for your baby. Some babies will want a couple of blankets to feel the heaviness, while others will want room to move freely. If you are worried the child will kick off the blankets and be cold at night, put the baby in a footed sleeper.

Sleep Little Baby

Quiet the room - At this age, noises will affect a child's ability to sleep. They tend to be stimulating to the more active and alert child. While typical household noise is usually fine, do what you can to limit sudden, loud sounds. Disconnect the doorbell so nobody will ring it, oil the hinges on squeaky doors, put the dog outside if it tends to bark and turn your cell phone to vibrate. Every child is different! Your child may sleep better with some background music or water running. If you discover your child is struggling to stay asleep or fall asleep, try playing some very low background noise.

Winding down - Toddlers are very active and can automatically switch gears when they are told it is bedtime. You need to start the bedtime ritual well in advance. Give the child at least an hour to start transitioning from playtime to sleep time. It could be something like this, dinner, bath, story time and then bed.

Cry it out - This does not mean the child is left in his bed to cry for hours on end. The child is learning coping mechanisms at this age. If you put the child to bed after the standard ritual and he still struggles a bit to wind down, leave him be. Let the child lie in his bed for a bit. The child may cry a little, call for you or even talk to himself. Stay out of the room and let the child try and work through it alone. This can be a little difficult at first. The first time you do this, it may take 15 minutes, the second and third nights it may take 10 minutes. If you see progress, you will know it is working. If it is difficult to hear your child cry, try to keep yourself busy. Wash the dishes, fold the laundry or try and watch television to keep your mind off the crying baby.

Cool and comfortable - We all sleep a little better when the room is slightly cool. There is a line between cool and comfortable and too cold. Turn down the thermostat a couple of degrees so the child doesn't get too warm and end up waking up. You will find you sleep better in a cooler environment as well.

2 years to 5 years

By now, your toddler is capable of going to sleep and sleeping through the night. Capable does not always mean it happens. You will need to create an ideal sleeping environment, including a ritual

Sleep Little Baby

that gets your child ready to sleep for at least 10 hours. You will want to make sure the child has used the restroom, gotten a last drink of water and is prepared to sleep without interruption. Sometimes, it isn't the getting to bed that is the problem with children of this age. It is the staying in bed that interrupts the child's sleep and yours.

Comfort - Make your child's room and bed as cozy as possible. You want to create the perfect environment for sleeping. Special sheets and blankets are one way you can make it more inviting. A big kid bed (toddler bed) with rails is often enough encouragement for the child to go to bed alone. Tuck in the child, turn on a night light and leave the room. Make sure the room is dark and quiet. Room darkening shades are very helpful during the summer when early bedtimes mean it is still daylight outside.

Story time - Your toddler will have the ability to get up out of bed as often he pleases. You can help encourage the child to stay in bed by spending 5 to 10 minutes in the room with the child while he lies in bed. Read a story, talk about the day for a few minutes or sing lullabies while the child lies down. This will make the child feel more comfortable about the pending separation. The child needs to feel safe in his bed and with you spending a little time helping him make the transition, he will.

Avoiding nightmares/bad dreams - Toddlers are beginning to develop an active imagination at this stage. Your child may get out of bed and come running for you if he has bad dreams. If it happens regularly, your sleep schedule can be thrown off. Monitor television programs that could be causing the dreams. Bedtime stories should be free of monsters, dragons or other fictional creatures that are making their way into your child's dreams. If a bad dream does awaken the child, soothe the child and let him know it is okay. Avoid telling the child it isn't real, because in their minds it is very real. Don't spend 30 minutes explaining bad dreams. Lie with the child a few minutes and reassure him before leaving the room.

Reassurance - If your child is new to a toddler bed, he may feel a little insecure. If the child calls out for you every time you leave the room or gets out of bed and follows you, you will need to reassure him everything is okay. Insist the child stays in bed. Check on the

Sleep Little Baby

child every 5 minutes or so. He will see you are still there and will feel better. The next day, you can check in every 8 minutes and slowly make the time intervals longer. This helps assure the child you are nearby if he needs you.

Keeping the child in bed - There are plenty of creative excuses for getting out of bed. The need to use the potty, the need for a drink or whatever excuses the child can come up with. When this happens, turn the child around and put him back in bed. Tuck him in without getting into a discussion. You may need to do this repeatedly the first night, but it will gradually decrease as the child learns you will not be swayed. Do not get angry and shout at the child. Stay calm and simply put him back in bed.

Chapter 9: More Health Tips for Mother and Child

This chapter essentially contains three sections, namely, a section on postpartum health, one of the more important yet neglected aspects of motherhood; a section on how to choose the right pediatrician for your baby, which is crucial in determining the health of your little one throughout his formative years; and a section on other related health issues that you should consider.

Postpartum Health Management

One of the most common misconceptions about childbirth is that only the newborn baby requires adequate care and support upon birth. However, it is also important to take care of the mother who has just given birth, because she is also just as vulnerable to risks and even possible complications after giving birth. This is especially true if the mother does not seek nor undergo proper postpartum healthcare. In this section, we provide information regarding postpartum health, including an overview of what the postpartum period is, how postpartum healthcare should be managed, and the goals a new mother and her doctor should set for herself six weeks after giving birth. Armed with such information, mothers should be able to manage their health and well----being which, in turn, will allow them to fully take care of their newborn baby.

The Postpartum Period

A lot of people believe that the pregnancy timeline ends once a baby is born. However, as a new mother, you should continue to closely monitor your health, with support from healthcare professionals, to ensure that your postpartum health is being properly evaluated and managed.

The postpartum period begins immediately after delivery and lasts up to eight weeks after childbirth. During this crucial period, you may experience discomfort, uneasiness and even complications, which should immediately be reported to your doctor. In fact, it is highly recommended that you have your postpartum appointment with your doctor at about 6 or 8 weeks after giving birth to your baby.

Obviously, the postpartum period is an important part of the pregnancy timeline, because this is the time at which you (your mind and your body) are adjusting to changes after delivery and to your changing roles as a new mother as well. How you cope with motherhood largely depends on whether or not you will be able to meet your postpartum health goals (more on this will be discussed later). For now, let us take a look at the basic objectives of a successful postpartum period transition. During the postpartum period, the following goals should be met:

- Proper management of the mother's physical, psychological, and emotional health;
- Fostering of healthy and supportive interactions among the mother, her partner, and their baby;
- Provision of sufficient knowledge that shall allow the mother to properly take care of her newborn baby; and
- Development and improvement of the mother's parenting skills.

During the postpartum period, the physiological changes you will experience include fluctuating blood pressure, excessive blood discharge, shifting of your internal organs to their normal positions, increased demand for rest, and so on. As for the psychological and emotional changes, you may experience increased feelings of exhaustion, depression, guilt, inability to cope, and so on.

If left unchecked, these changes can develop into possible complications that will ultimately harm your overall health. Thus, it is important to pay close attention to your health during the postpartum period.

Things to Expect After Giving Birth

As mentioned earlier, your body goes through tremendous changes after giving birth, and part of successful postpartum healthcare is to ensure that you are able to handle these changes and manage them safely with the help of your doctor and your family. Just as your body experiences drastic changes while being pregnant with your baby, drastic changes after giving birth can also be expected. This is because your body is attempting to get back to its normal shape and condition before it changed to accommodate a baby inside. This subsection provides a list of what you should expect after giving birth.

Vaginal discharge

Immediately after delivery and many weeks after that, you will experience varying degrees of vaginal discharge or what is called lochia. While your baby is still inside your womb, he is enveloped by layers of tissue and blood that lined the uterus. When your baby comes out, this lining will be shed, like menstruation. However, lochia is different in that you will expel large amounts of lochia that range in color from bright red to yellow or white. The bleeding is heavier and has a bright red color for the first three or four days after delivery, then turns pink, then dark red/brown, and finally white or yellow as the weeks pass. Lochia is shed gradually but can be discharged in clots when making sudden movements. It can even turn bright red again with excessive activities.

Cramping

Cramping, which is also called "afterpain," is common among women who just gave birth. When you experience cramping, this means that your uterus is contracting back to its normal size. Severe cramping can be experienced especially after two or three days of delivery and eventually lessens in about a week. It is said that afterpains are usually worse for seconds or third----time mothers because their uterus requires much more effort to get back to its old size, compared with first----time mothers who still have muscle tone in their uterus. In addition, breastfeeding moms also report cramping. This is because the baby's sucking initiates the release of the hormone called oxytocin, which then triggers contractions in the uterus that lead to cramping.

Swelling

Also called "edema," swelling is a common accompaniment of pregnancy. However, swelling can also occur after a mother gives birth. Swelling after childbirth is often due to the body's retention of excessive fluids a few weeks before you gave birth. Thus, during the postpartum period, you will still experience swelling, usually 2 days to a week after delivery. Should swelling persist after a week, or if swelling is accompanied by severe headache and pain in the extremities, then you should call your doctor's attention for possible high blood pressure. Meanwhile, if only one leg continues to swell, with excessive pain, you may have what is called "deep vein thrombosis." In this case, immediate medical attention is also required.

Problems in urination

In relation to your body's need to expel all remaining fluids that have been retained during pregnancy, you may experience excessive urination or even temporary urinary incontinence. This is because your kidney is working double time to remove excess liquid from your system and restore it to its pre----pregnancy state. For those who have had an episiotomy, urinating for the first few days after delivery can be terribly painful. Nevertheless, the pain will also go away after some time. In addition, due to the damaged ligaments and muscles in your crotch area, you may also find it difficult to urinate. However, this reflex will be back to normal in as early as one week. For faster recovery, Kegel exercises are recommended so that the mother can regain control of her muscles in that region of her body.

Perspiration

Similar to excessive urination described above, your body also gets rid of excessive fluids through your sweat glands. Hence, perspiration is also a common experience a few days after giving birth.

Constipation

This is one of the most inconvenient experiences any new mother has after delivery. Postpartum constipation is due to several reasons. First, the abdominal muscles that have been severely stretched during pregnancy have yet to function normally a few days after delivery. Second, your intestines may not yet be able to operate in the same way that they have before you got pregnant. Since this can be quite painful especially for a mother who has had episiotomy, it is suggested that you use a stool softener. At the same time, you can also follow a strict diet consisting of fresh fruits and vegetables, lots of water, and foods that are rich in fiber. At the same time, Kegel exercises can also be done to gain full control of the muscles associated with bowel movement.

Soreness

The sensitive area between the rectum and the vagina is called the "perineum," which usually becomes sore and extremely painful, especially because it is stretched and torn and then stitched up during normal delivery. To relieve soreness, ice packs are usually placed over the area about 12 to 24 hours after once the perineum is stitched up. To eliminate possible infections, the area should be kept clean and dry. Once the stitches are dissolved, soreness lessens for a period of about 1 to 2 weeks after giving birth.

Postpartum Healthcare Goals

According to the Association of Reproductive Health Professionals, proper postpartum healthcare management requires that you and your doctor set goals that not only monitor your progress six weeks after giving birth but also facilitates quicker and safer transition back to your pre---pregnancy state. The so----called Six----Week Postpartum Health Goals include the following: Weight Loss, Balanced Nutrition, Physical Examination, and Provision of Information on Sexuality, Contraception, and Emotional Adjustment.

Weight loss

The goal of losing weight has got to be the most common among all mothers who have just given birth. Women pack on a lot of pounds during pregnancy so it requires a lot of work. Fortunately, this is a manageable goal with proper diet and exercise. However, before starting on an exercise routine, get clearance from your doctor first.

Nutrition

To facilitate safe weight loss of about 5 lbs per month, also consider consuming around 1,800 calories a day, mainly though foods rich in iron and protein (lean beef, seafood), low----fat dairy products, and green, leafy vegetables. Taking nutritional supplements, especially those that augment your iron and calcium intake, is also recommended.

Physical examination

After birth, you must be raring to get back to your normal routines. However, you need to have your regular physical examinations to ensure that your body is in top condition and to avoid possible complications. During your physical examination, you may ask your doctor about related concerns you may have regarding your vaginal discharge, soreness from breastfeeding, problems with bowel movement and constipation, appearance of varicose veins, proper healing of your perineum

Sleep Little Baby

(for those who had natural childbirth) or abdominal wound (for those who had a C----section).

Information on sexuality and contraception

One of the goals of postpartum healthcare management is to you ease back into your pre----pregnancy routines, one of which is resuming sexual activities with your partner. Sexual desires soon come back a few weeks after giving birth. For those who opt not to breastfeed their baby, ovulation may occur in as early as 45 days after giving birth. Thus, it is important to explore this aspect of postpartum healthcare with your doctor. For example, when exactly will you be fertile again? Are you considering family planning options? When can you safely have sex with your partner again? How can you reduce discomfort when having sex? These are important concerns so do not be embarrassed to ask your doctor about them.

Emotional adjustment

Aside from dealing with physiological changes in your body, you also have to deal with your emotional and mental condition after giving birth. Many mothers with newborn babies have to rest and recuperate for some time at home. This seclusion, along with the added tasks of taking care of a baby round----the----clock may result in feelings of isolation, severe exhaustion, crankiness, moodiness, nervousness, loss, and so on. In severe cases, such feelings may lead to postpartum depression, thus, it is important that you express your concerns with your doctor. Some of the things you can do to minimize these "baby blues" are as follows:

- Touch base with families and friends;
- Set some "me time" within the day (like taking a long, luxurious bath while your baby is sleeping);
- Join forums for newborn moms; and
- Go on brisk walks outside (with or without your baby) if weather conditions are good.

Possible Complications

The common symptoms experienced by women after giving birth have been discussed above. To recap, these may include vaginal discharge, pain and soreness in the perineum, difficulty in bowel movement and urination, as well as swelling, to name a few. While these are expected, you should also watch out for complications that may arise when these are left unaddressed. Generally, the following indicators serve as red flags that you should see your doctor immediately:

- Extreme pain and swelling in your lower extremities
- Persistent pain in the perineum
- Excessive bleeding or discharge
- Sore and overly swollen breasts
- Burning sensation while urinating
- Vomiting
- Headache and nausea
- Feelings of depression and lack of interest in taking care of your baby

Let us now take a look at some possible complications you may have during the postpartum period

Uterine infection

After giving birth, the placenta is supposed to be discharged naturally about 20 minutes after delivery. If some parts are not expelled and remain in the uterus, this can lead to uterine infection. Symptoms of infection include discharge with a very foul odor, extremely high WBC count, very high fever, rapid heart rate, and swollen uterus. If left untreated, this could lead to toxic shock, and possibly, death.

Hemorrhage

Though it occurs in very few cases of delivery, hemorrhage is the third common cause of maternal death. Hemorrhage may arise in cases of multiple births, lengthy labor period, and uterine infection. This complication can also be due to damage/tears in the cervix and uterus as well as the failure of the uterus to contract (and expel the placenta) following delivery. Doctors can immediately treat hemorrhage should it occur at the hospital, but upon discharge, the mother should immediately report if hemorrhage occurs at home.

Infection of the kidney

A kidney infection may occur when the bladder becomes infected and spreads bacteria to the kidney. Accompanying symptoms of kidney infection include frequent urination, burning sensation while peeing, lower back pain, and very high fever. Again, the mother should report these symptoms to her doctor so that antibiotics (oral or IV) can be immediately prescribed.

Infection from a C----section

This kind of infection usually occurs when the mother fails to follow instructions regarding proper care of a C----section incision. You may be infected if you observe the following symptoms: the wound fails to heal after the prescribed period, presence of pus, the surrounding skin is swollen, and so on.

Mastitis

Mastitis or breast infection can also arise during the postpartum period. This is usually indicated by swelling, tenderness, and reddened patches on the breast. As with other kinds of infection, you may experience very high fever, nausea, vomiting, and chills. Your doctor will simply prescribe antibiotics as a form of treatment. Although mastitis does not affect the quality of your breast milk, do check with your doctor if you can continue breastfeeding your baby while under medication.

Postpartum depression

Postpartum depression is one of the most cited psychological complications that may occur after giving birth. It affects 10% to 20% of mothers who have recently given birth and is accompanied by symptoms such as anxiety, despair, lack of energy, fear, lack of interest in one's baby, hallucinations, and even the desire to harm those around. Postpartum depression is often attributed to the combined effects of physical trauma due to childbirth, exhaustion/lack of sleep, and changing hormonal levels after giving birth.

While it is normal to experience "baby blues," such feeling can progress to postpartum depression or even postpartum psychosis if left untreated. If you observe the following symptoms, then it is important to speak with your doctor right away:

- No energy or drive to do anything;
- Insomnia;
- Migraines and heart palpitations
- Overeating
- Restlessness and irritability
- Constantly depressed and sad
- Problems in making decisions or being extremely worried about the baby
- Not having any interest in the baby
- Having thoughts of harming oneself or the baby Certainly, the easiest way to get rid of postpartum depression is by actively taking steps to avoid having feelings such as those listed above. You can ask your family and friends to help you with this as well as seek professional guidance from your doctor.

Remember that postpartum depression can only be treated properly once you report it to the doctor. Thus, do not be embarrassed about having these feelings. Be open and seek help so that you can live a healthier life after giving birth and take proper care of your baby.

How to Choose the Right Doctor for Your Baby

The previous subsection discussed postpartum healthcare management, which provides various information and ways, by which a mother can take care of herself after giving birth. In

Sleep Little Baby

this second subsection of the chapter, we will introduce another related aspect of motherhood, which is finding the right pediatrician for your baby.

It is very important to find the right doctor for your baby for several reasons. First, you will be making well----baby visits to the doctor's clinic on a regular basis for the first year of your baby's life and even beyond that. Second, your baby's doctor will be the prime source of information for anything related to your baby's health. Third, your baby's pediatrician will be partly responsible for the decisions you will make regarding your baby. For these reasons, you have to be careful in making this decision. In the following, let us take a look at some useful tips in choosing the right doctor for your baby

Tip #1 – Identify Your Preferences

Identifying the right doctor for your baby may seem like an overwhelming and daunting task, especially for first----time parents. As mentioned above, it is an important decision that is hinged upon several factors. Among these, your preferences should play a great role in such a choice. First of all, you will be personally communicating with the doctor and will be dealing with him/her for the next year or so of your baby's life.

On the one hand, some parents would want a doctor whose expertise is on taking care of babies and young children; hence, a pediatrician would be the right choice. This choice is advantageous because a pediatrician can adeptly handle medical issues related to infants and babies. On the other hand, some parents prefer a family doctor or GP who can treat the whole family from birth. This choice is beneficial as it ensures continuity of care and consistency in reading a baby's medical issues.

In choosing a doctor for your baby, other preference points can include the following:

- Whether the doctor is easy to talk to and is approachable
- Whether the doctor interacts well with babies and young kids
- Whether the doctor is updated in the latest trends in medical treatment
- Whether the doctor invites questions from the parents
- Whether the doctor is careful in explaining medical issues in layman's terms
- Whether the clinic is comfortable, accessible, and employs helpful staff
- Whether the doctor is available even after clinic hours

Your ultimate choice may also depend on whether you have the same parenting style as the doctor or whether he or she is highly recommended by friends and families. These points shall be discussed in the following subsections.

Tip #2 – Seek Referrals From Friends And Family Members

In choosing the right doctor for your baby, the most logical approach in coming up with a list of candidates is to seek referrals from friends and families. There are no other people you would entrust with your very own life except your family members and close friends. Thus, it is only right that you seek their help when it comes to making this important decision for your baby.

Do not underestimate the power of your very own network in finding the right doctor. In this case, family member and friends can provide a wealth of information not just for possible candidates, but a whole range of suggestions and tips to help you narrow down your list of candidates. Another benefit of seeking referrals from them is having the knowledge that they have actually benefited from the services of the doctors they are recommending. Thus, you can learn valuable lessons from their actual experiences.

Aside from family and friends, however, you can also ask other trusted people in your network, such as your OB, co----workers, and even your neighbors. Just remember to take the good suggestions and integrate them into your working list based on the preference points discussed in Tip#1.

Other considerations to help you come up with a list of candidates are as follows:

- Whether the doctor is provided by your insurance network
- Whether the doctor has been certified by the American Academy of Pediatrics
- (AAP), which provides a list of certified doctors in its website

Tip #3 – Set Up An Appointment

Once you have come up with a short list of candidates, the next step is to talk to the doctors personally by setting appointments with each of them is possible. Being able to talk to the doctors face to face can help you come up with better decision since there are some things you can determine, while speaking to them face to face rather than just checking out their credentials in their websites on home pages. By paying the doctor a visit, you will be able to gauge the doctor's personality, the way he/she interacts with his little patients and their parents, the way he provides quality service and so on.

To be able to set up an appointment, you can either ask for their numbers through the referral or by checking out their websites, and then setting up an appointment by phone or by email. Whether the personnel who receives your queries and requests is polite and helpful and whether the process is a difficult or easy one, can also determine your decision. A staff member who is rude and inefficient can only give you a hard time setting up future appointments with the doctors with whom they are working.

Once you have successfully booked an appointment, you can then draw up your list of questions. Do not, however, ask these as if you are interviewing the doctor. Ask your prepared questions discreetly but directly. Some of the possible questions to ask are as follows:

- Are you available for consultation beyond clinic hours?
- Can you patiently and comprehensively explain medical issues to parents?
- Are you willing to work with the parents in coming up with a specific well----baby program for each baby?

Once you have met the candidate doctors in your list, you can now make a decision based on the information you have gathered and also on your general assessment of the doctors with whom you have set up an appointment. In making an overall assessment, perhaps it's also a good idea to choose the doctor with whom you feel a connection. This is what the final tip is about.

Tip #4 – Check For Compatibility

You and your chosen doctor shall become partners in ensuring that proper healthcare is given to your baby. This doctor should not only be adept at providing such service, but also somebody with whom you have a connection. Sometimes, the interaction between parents and their child's doctor exceeds beyond professional boundaries. As with any partnership, it is important that the doctor you will eventually choose is someone who you see as an excellent working partner for the first few years of your child's life.

Do You Have The Same Views on Parenting in General?

Sleep Little Baby

Working with a doctor, someone to whom you will entrust your child's health, involves making crucial decisions at several periods of your child's development stage. In this case, it is important that the doctor you will choose shares the same views you have about several things related to child rearing.

For example, does the doctor encourage breastfeeding? Is he for or against co----sleeping? If he is against co----sleeping, is he in favor of the "crying it out method?" Does he have a preference for natural or synthetic medicines? What are his views regarding vaccination? What about weaning? What are his thoughts on circumcision? Identifying answers to these questions will help you gauge whether you share the same parenting principles as your candidate doctor.

In summary, this chapter deals with the two most important players involved in your baby's delivery—you and your baby. In the first part of the chapter, the book discusses postpartum healthcare management and the related information, such as an overview of the postpartum period, the postpartum healthcare goals, and the possible complications that may arise. Meanwhile, the second part of the chapter presents useful tips of how to choose the right doctor for your baby. Mainly, you should choose a doctor who has been referred by families and friends, someone whose practice agrees well with your parenting principles, and whose personality complements yours. By taking care of yourself and your baby, both of you shall continue to live healthy lives together.

Chapter 10: Analyze

Now that you've done all you can to ensure your baby's success, he or she should have a great night of healthy sleep, right?

We wish! As any parent will tell you, even after all precautions have been taken, a baby might still have trouble sleeping. Many people feel that the reasons a baby doesn't sleep are inexplicable, just part of 'being a baby,' and not something they can do anything about.

Thankfully, that isn't the case. When babies don't sleep well, there is always an underlying cause. Using your analytical skills, you can learn to identify the underlying causes of your baby's sleepless nights, and once you have an understanding of why your baby doesn't sleep, you can start to problem-solve how to help get them on track. This is a step that you will be taking throughout your baby's development into a healthy child.

Let's go over some common obstacles that might be interfering with your baby's sleep and learn how to overcome them.

Overtiredness

If your baby is overtired, they are unlikely to sleep well at night. Even in the best of circumstances, there will be days when your baby's routine is disrupted and they miss some of that important napping time. If this happens, be prepared to take steps to help your baby fall asleep and stay asleep once evening hits.

Try this: If possible, give your baby a short make-up nap at an appropriate point in the day. If it's too late and overtiredness can't be avoided, take extra care to help your baby relax before bed, by turning down the lights, engaging in soothing routines, or giving them a gentle bath. Try to keep their environment quiet by turning off the TV and radio. You may need to hold or rock your baby to sleep to give them an extra boost, but be wary of making this a habit.

Sleep Little Baby

Distraction

Outside distractions can be another obstacle to healthy baby sleep. Sounds, lights, toys, and visual stimuli can all keep your baby from dropping off into slumber. Older babies and toddlers are more easily distracted by their surroundings, but babies of any age will benefit from a distraction-free environment.

Try this: Make sure that your baby's sleeping place is located in a place that can be cut off from unnecessary noise and light, such as that from a TV. Remove toys from in and around the crib or bed. If you use a nightlight, make sure that the room remains dark enough for sleepy eyes to let go of the visual stimulus all around them.

Overstimulation

Overstimulation can be another culprit blocking your baby's way to sleep. Overstimulation can come in many forms, sometimes even from your own attempts to soothe!

Try this: Avoid rowdy play or getting your baby 'wound-up' before bed. Create a calming night ritual and stick to it. Allow your baby to put himself back to sleep whenever possible; babies, just like adults, toss and turn and wake up briefly throughout the night. They don't always need your help to get back to sleep.

Hunger or Thirst

Crying is how your baby gets her needs met. Baby tummies are small. The younger your baby is, the more often that they will wake up in the night due to hunger or thirst.

Try this: If your baby is crying, check to see if they are hungry or thirsty. Often addressing these needs is all it takes to get them back to sleep. If your baby is still waking up hungry after 4-6 months, try adjusting their feeding schedule to make sure that they're getting enough to eat and drink. If the problem persists, bring it to the attention of your pediatrician.

Nightmares

Sleep Little Baby

Nightmares are dreams with disturbing content or emotions. If you've ever had one, you know just how frightening they can be! It's uncertain as to exactly when babies begin having nightmares, but it's thought that nightmares start to show up by your baby's first birthday. Since most dreaming happens during the second half of the night, this is when nightmares are most likely to occur.

No one is completely certain why nightmares happen, however they are usually linked to stress, illness, physical or mental/emotional discomfort, or pain. If your baby is ill, for example, you may find that they experience more nightmares. The same is true if they have a stressful day or experience separation anxiety in the hours leading up to bed time. If your baby wakes up from a nightmare, they may be distressed and have a difficult time falling back to sleep.

Try this: To calm your baby down after a nightmare, start by reassuring them of your presence. Speak in a soothing tone of voice and provide physical contact in the form of hugs or back rubs. Engage in familiar sleep routines such as rocking or walking. Stay in the room with them while they fall back to sleep.

Night terrors

Night terrors are more common in older children but may occur in toddlers as well. Babies may exhibit behavior resembling a night terror, however these may be classified as confusional arousals. To an observant parent, night terrors may appear to be like intense or extreme nightmares. When a baby or toddler experiences a night terror, they may sit up suddenly and start screaming, crying or shouting. They will appear to be experiencing intense fear and may be sweating or panting. Night terrors may last a few seconds or several minutes. The baby may or may not wake up after the night terror, and in either case will probably not remember that it has occurred. Because babies and toddlers are not aware that a night terror has happened, these are often more distressing for parents than for the baby himself.

Try this: If your baby or toddler experiences a night terror, don't try to wake them. The best thing that you can do is simply wait for the night terror to pass and watch out for any danger. Your baby probably won't realize you are there even if you do try to help. If your baby or toddler experiences night terrors, take some precautions to keep them safe, similar to those you would for sleepwalking.

Sleepwalking

Although sleepwalking usually occurs in children, your toddler has the potential to begin walking in her sleep as soon as she's learned how to do it while awake. If your toddler is sleepwalking, she may appear to be awake, or even speak to you, when in reality she is asleep and unaware of what is going on. Sleepwalking in and of itself need not reflect a disorder, however sleepwalking may lead to risky situations such as opening doors and wandering outside. It's important to take precautions if your toddler has this problem. Even if your toddler is still in the crib, they may try to climb out in their sleep, adding to the potential safety issues that surround this phenomenon.

Try this: Rather than trying to wake your sleepwalker up, gently guide him back to his bed or crib. Use baby gates to block stairs and areas of the house you don't want them wandering into. Keep windows and doors locked to prevent your toddler from opening them. Make sure that there are no hard or sharp objects around their sleeping space, and don't put them in beds or cribs that they may fall out of.

Bedwetting

As toddlers are still potty training, chances are high that your toddler's bedwetting is due to not yet having developed sufficient control. However, if you feel that your toddler's bedwetting is pathological, seek advice from your pediatrician. In the meantime, be patient as you help your toddler master a night without wetting the bed.

Try this: Reduce your toddler's fluid intake before bed, and remember to increase it during the day so that they still get enough to drink. Avoid caffeine and citrus juices as these can irritate the bladder. Don't punish your toddler if an accident happens—instead, use positive encouragement and rewards to make them feel good about success. In the event that your toddler simply isn't ready to control their bladder at night, consider letting them wear a pullup to bed even if they've graduated to 'big kid' underwear during the day.

Regression

Another important consideration to take into account as you analyze your baby's sleep is regression. Sometimes, a baby who has learned to fall asleep easily will suddenly begin having trouble dropping off. Other times, babies who have learned to sleep through the night will go back to waking up several times before morning. These types of regressions are normal, and are not necessarily a cause for alarm.

Many baby's go through a regression at around four months and again every four to six months thereafter. However, regression could happen at any time as your baby grows and develops and sleep patterns change. Regressions usually last between one and four weeks and may have no apparent cause.

You may feel frustrated if your baby experiences a regression. For tired parents, times like these can make it seem that all of your hard work to sleep train your baby has gone out the window. Take heart! By training your baby for healthy sleep, you are giving them a solid foundation for development.

Regressions are temporary, so don't stop the training just because your baby seems to have back slid. Continue to engage in the four steps outlined in this book as you and your baby work through the regression together. In a few weeks, things will usually be back on track until the next time.

Chapter 11: Teaching Your Baby the Art of Sleeping

It may seem like a silly notion to an adult who is sleep deprived and hoping for a solid night's rest, but you really need to teach your baby the art of sleeping. You had to learn at some point and now you need to teach your baby. As shocking as it may sound, it isn't always instinct. Sleep is a necessity, but learning the art of sleeping requires a bit of training.

Babies and toddlers are thrust into a big, strange world. They want to explore every inch of it. When they feel the pull of sleep trying to bring them down, it is only natural they would want to fight it in order to keep exploring. They want to stay awake so they can interact with mom, dad and their siblings. They likely feel they are going to miss out on something really spectacular if they give into their body's need for sleep. Haven't you ever stayed up late watching a television show even though you knew you were going to be tired the next day? Of course you have! It is essentially the same thing with little ones. They figure they don't really need all the sleep mom and dad keep insisting on.

You want to teach them that sleeping is a good thing. Making sleep an enjoyable activity will help sway their way of thinking. Although they won't understand solid reasoning like telling them they will feel better after they get a good night's rest, you can persuade them to sleep in their bed by making it a pleasant experience.

Differentiating Between Night and Day

Your first goal is teaching your baby night and day. When you get your baby home from the hospital, you will quickly realize they have no regard for when the household is sleeping and when it is awake. You can start training your baby in the first few days of life. Here's how it works:

1-Place your baby's bed near a window. Do your best to get up at the same time every day. If it is 5 am or 8 am, stick with it. If the baby is

Sleep Little Baby

sleeping, open the window to let the light in or turn on the light. This will help baby to see daylight means awake time.

2-At bedtime and naptime, darken the room. Darkness means sleep. Your baby will start to grasp this concept fairly early on if you stick to a routine.

3-During daytime feedings, play with your baby's feet, talk with the baby and keep the lights on. Nighttime feedings will be in low-light, with no playing, talking or giggling. The child will start to learn the difference between the feedings. Nighttime feedings will be shorter and you and the baby will get more sleep.

Rituals and Routines

The first three months of your baby's life are going to be pretty much on his schedule. Although you can start "training" the baby to sleep by nursing, bathing and shutting down the lights as part of the bedtime routine, know that at this young age, the baby needs frequent feedings. Every baby is different, but on average, a child will only go 2 to 4 hours between feedings. Trying to establish a set routine is a little difficult. If you typically go to bed at 9, start your baby's bedtime routine around 8, depending on how long it takes. If you need to bathe, feed, burp and then rock to sleep, you are looking at a good hour. Don't start the process at 9 and become frustrated when the baby doesn't fall asleep until 10.

Experiment early on with various bedtime rituals. A word of caution about lengthy rituals, once you have established a ritual, it will likely carry through the child's early years. If you are not up for a 45-minute ritual every night for the next several years, don't start it now.

No-Cry Method versus Cry it Out

You have likely heard arguments on both sides of the debate. Some experts and well-meaning friends and family members, will tell you to put the baby in bed and let him cry until he eventually falls asleep. Others will tell you leaving your baby alone and crying is a betrayal and your baby will not learn to distrust you. Both sides have valid arguments. What it comes down to is what feels right to you. Are you okay leaving your baby to cry for 15 to 30 minutes? If not, don't feel

Sleep Little Baby

as if you are "spoiling" your baby if you can't do it. However, you will want to give your baby a chance to soothe himself. Here are some tips that are in line with both methods:

- When the baby is crying, leave him in bed, but gently rub his tummy or stand next to the crib while singing or humming.
- When the baby cries, pick him up, soothe him and put him right back in bed.
- Establish key sounds/words like "shhh" or "sleepy time" to soothe the child into sleep.
- Stand outside the door or put a chair outside the door of baby's room, when he starts crying, talk to him from the door, but don't go in the room.

Your baby is of course going to be comforted by the sound of your voice and being able to be close to you. It isn't surprising that some babies are a little hesitant to fall asleep if they know they will be separated from their parents. You want the baby to know sleeping is safe and you will be there to take care of their needs no matter what. Soothing the baby when he is in bed will help him understand he isn't alone or abandoned.

It will take some time for the baby to learn sleeping is a wonderful thing. Parents will need to have patience and realize that training a baby to sleep has its ups and downs, but it will happen eventually. The key is learning your baby's personality and what works. Once you have discovered what works best for your baby, it is all about consistency. Allow yourself a minimum of a full week of following a consistent routine to train your baby how to sleep. Don't give up on the second or third night because it isn't working. You need to give it some time before you move on to the next method.

You can help your child feel tired and ready to welcome sleep by keeping him busy during his awake time. When the weather allows, get the child outside to explore his new world. Babies who crawl or walk will love running just to run. You don't want to over-stimulate the child, but you want the child to get all of his exploring done during his waking hours. For infants and newborns, tummy time, feeding and spending time chatting with mom and dad is plenty of stimulation. Look for signs the child is wearing down and start on the bedtime routine. If it is 20 minutes earlier than usual, that is okay. Your baby will do best when he is put to sleep when he is tired and not over tired.

Common sleepy signs include:

- Yawning
- Slowing down - crawlers may prefer to just lay on the floor while walkers will sit down
- Rubbing the eyes
- Fussiness
- Breast fed baby may "root" when being held

Do your best to watch for the signs. You want to put the baby to bed when he is still awake, but on the verge of falling asleep. It will make your job much easier and will help teach the child he can fall asleep on his own.

Naps—Good or Bad

You have probably heard the reasoning you need to keep the baby awake during the day so he will sleep through the night. No naps would mean the baby is so exhausted by bedtime he will fall right to sleep and not wake up until the next morning, right? WRONG!

We have already discussed the importance of sleep for your child. A child is not physically capable of sleeping 12 hours straight. Their little tummies need food more often than an adult. Depriving your child of a nap or two during the day is doing nothing but making your life more difficult and making the child cranky. You absolutely must do what you can to get your baby to nap during the day.

Without adequate sleep, your child will struggle to go to sleep at night. When he does fall asleep, it will likely be a restless sleep that will keep you up anyway. Babies need plenty of sleep in order to be healthy and develop properly. By reasoning the baby will be so tired he will just pass out will backfire! A child who is overtired will lack the coping mechanisms needed to soothe himself to sleep.

Newborn to 6 months

Sleep Little Baby

Your newborn will likely sleep off and on throughout the night and day. Setting up established nap times is very difficult at this age because the child is growing and his needs are changing. Your baby will only be awake for 4 to 8 hours during the entire 24-hour period. Ideally, you would prefer those waking hours to be during the day, but it doesn't always happen that way. Do your best to put your baby down for several naps throughout the day to keep him rested and more able to handle longer sleeping periods at night.

6 months to a 1 year

At this stage, your baby's feeding needs are not quite as demanding. You can expect the child to start sleeping for longer blocks of time at night, which means more awake time during the day. A typical schedule for a child of this age is bed at 8 and awake at 6 with two naps during the day. Expect the naps to last about 2 hours each. The first nap may be at 10 a.m.. The baby wakes up eats lunch and plays for a few hours before another nap around 3 or 4. The baby will sleep a couple of hours, wake up, eat dinner, play and be ready for bedtime.

1 to 3 years

Babies at this age are typically able to sleep through the night and will likely only need one nap during the day. Nap times vary, but average anywhere from one to three hours. The nap should be timed so it is about halfway through the baby's waking hours. After lunch is a good time depending on what the child's schedule is.

3 to 5 years

Each child will differ in the amount of sleep they need. There are plenty of preschoolers who will do just fine without a nap, while others absolutely must have one. The child's nap needs will typically depend on the quality of sleep they are getting at night. You will need to watch the child and look for signs of sleepiness. If the child is tired, put him down for a nap. It may not be needed every day. It is important a child does not become overly tired. If you have had a busy day running at the park for hours, the child will likely be tired

Sleep Little Baby

and need a nap to get through the rest of the day. Use your best judgment.

Overall, naps are absolutely necessary not only for the child's health and development, but for your own mental health. Taking care of babies and toddlers is a big job. You cannot leave them alone for a minute and have to be on high alert all the time. Nap time gives you some time to relax or even catch a little sleep yourself.

The trick is timing the naps for your baby or toddler so they don't interfere with the long block of nighttime sleep. Your child will need anywhere from 2 to 4 hours to wind down after waking from a nap. If your scheduled bedtime is at 8, naptime should be over by 4 or 5 at the latest. It can take several weeks before you figure out the right routine for your child. The child may fight naps every day, every single nap, but as long as you are persistent and consistent, they will realize there is no escaping the nap.

You will likely need to employ some of the sleep solutions mentioned throughout this book. Darken the room, put on some quiet music, rock the child or whatever has become part of the sleep routine to help them understand that it is time to rest for a bit.

Sleep Little Baby
Chapter 12: Safety

There are several aspects to putting your baby to bed safely, and many of them will be included below. While guidelines and other advice may be based on scientific findings, many people manage to ignore them and continue on to have a happy, healthy baby. For many others, though, what is the point in taking that risk? If you can minimize any risk to your baby, shouldn't you do so? For instance, there are some parents who have an issue with the idea that they cannot decorate their baby's crib. Many doctors have said that if you want to decorate something, decorate the baby's room. Your baby's crib is designed to be a safety device. Use it that way.

By eliminating things that could become loose and cause an issue for a baby who lacks full motor skills, you are ensuring that these things will not be a problem. How can you worry about a giant stuffed bear with a ribbon possibly smothering your child in the crib if it is not there? No errant strings can cause an issue from a blanket that is not in the crib. Or if you are worried about your baby remaining warm throughout the night, there is a ton of adorable options available from sleep sacks to footed pajamas.

The American Academy of Pediatrics has successfully cut the rate of crib death, also known as SIDS, down by a staggering 50% by implementing a few guidelines. While most parents have heard these statistics and facts, it is important to stay up to date as there is always going to be improvements and adjustments made. For example, the minimization of the amount of space between crib slats eliminated the need for baby bumpers, which cut down on two causes of infant death.

Thankfully, after these points were made, many babies and their parents no longer had the concern of the baby getting their head stuck in the sides of the crib. Further, the removal of the bumpers eliminated the possibility of suffocation. And the elimination of cribs with drop-down sides has also improved the statistics of babies injured while in their beds or the older toddlers who have learned to climb out.

Sleep Little Baby

In the interest of the welfare of all of our precious babies, here are the guidelines for putting babies to bed safely. Some of them may not seem directly related, but we all know how important our children are. Let's keep them safe any way we can. At the top of the list of tips to decrease the risk of SIDS for your baby is breastfeeding. According to a study that was published in the June 2011 issue of Pediatrics, children who were exclusively breastfed had over a 50% decreased risk of SIDS. There are many different speculations as to why this is, including the number of antibodies that breastfed babies receive. It has also been noted in speculation that breastfed babies are easier to awaken, which is a very significant point as babies who have difficulties being woken up have been found to be more prone to SIDS.

For the many mothers who may be on a particular medication that does not allow for them to breastfeed, do not be discouraged. There are plenty of additional measures you can take to ensure you reduce your baby's risk as much as possible. Adherence to vaccination schedules is also highly emphasized since research published in 2007 in the Vaccine journal showed that infants who were properly immunized also had a nearly 50% lower chance of SIDS. Surprisingly, pacifiers have also been linked to reducing the risk of SIDS. Appropriate pacifiers can be used at nap time and bedtime.

Additional guidelines include laying your baby in a sturdy, firm crib covered only with a fitted sheet; no blankets, pillows, or stuffed animals should be in the crib. Why? By eliminating pillows, there are no allergens or loose threads, and the baby's head will not sink into it. Without things in the crib, you will have a clear view of your baby with the baby monitor. And as your baby gets older and the twitches turn to fidgeting or playing with their fingers, you do not have to worry about them possibly wrapping something around their head or their limbs and cutting off circulation. Also, it is better to avoid the use of foam wedges and sleep positioners.

Babies should be laid down to sleep on their backs every time they go to sleep. Now, you may be concerned about a flattened head (also known as positional plagiocephaly) due to your baby spending so much of the day in this position. If this concerns you, consider using

Sleep Little Baby

supervised tummy time to keep them awake and engaged during the daytime, which will help enforce your sleep schedule and allow you to bond with your baby. While some babies love to be swaddled and sleep very well that way, not every baby is a fan. For those babies who like to fidget, a sleep sack can be a cute and cozy alternative to a blanket. A footed pajama is also a good choice. For those whose babies love being swaddled but cannot quite get the snug, secure wrapping correct right away, there are plenty of swaddling blankets available.

Safety is a very important factor to ensure that both you and your baby have a good night's sleep. Let's talk about a few of the important factors that will contribute to your baby's safety when it comes to sleeping.

- Sleeping Position – It is important that newborns sleep on their back. Recent studies have shown that babies who sleep on their backs rather than their tummies have a lower risk of SIDS.

As babies grow older and learn to roll over, many babies will roll around and sleep on their sides or even on their tummies. Once they can roll around on their own, doctors and pediatricians say that you do not have to worry about how they sleep, but you should still always put them to bed on their backs. If they then roll over, that's fine.

- Firm Sleeping Surface – It is extremely important that your baby has a firm surface to sleep on in order to avoid suffocation. Suffocation can happen easily if you allow your baby to fall asleep in his car seat for long periods of time like overnight. Obviously he'll sleep in his car seat when you are out driving around town, and that's okay, but you never want to let his car seat replace his crib or mattress. It is too easy for his head to fall forward, cutting off the air flow through his windpipe. Even if he falls asleep in the car while driving, you should be checking on him often to make sure that this does not happen.

- Remove All Loose Objects from the Crib – Especially as your newborn becomes a little more mobile in her crib, you'll want to make sure there are no loose objects in the crib that she could pull over her face or could roll into, causing her to suffocate during the night. Sometimes a baby rolls and then doesn't realize the need to roll away or can't figure out how to roll again. A stuffed animal, extra blanket, etc. could all be dangerous objects of concern for your newborn in this situation.

- Do Not Cover Your Baby's Head – Perhaps this goes without saying, but even placing an extra blanket around your baby's head to keep him warm may get pulled over his head throughout the course of the night. Even young babies will move their arms and legs some and can get tangled in things if they are too close to their head. If that happens and the extra blanket gets pulled up and over his head, it could possibly suffocate him or even overheat him. It is vital that you think ahead about all the possibilities when doing anything with your newborn.

- Implement Tummy Time – Simply lay your baby down on the carpet and on her tummy during the day and keep a close eye on her. Tummy time allows your baby to start developing the muscles in her neck and arms that will help her roll around and away from things. This helps her immensely with her safety since when she gets into a dangerous situation, she now has the ability to roll in the opposite direction.

Often when little ones get themselves too close to a blanket or stuffed animal, they know they want to roll away, but they don't know how. They have the survival instincts to know the situation is bad, but they don't know what to do. By helping them develop the muscles to roll around through tummy time, they learn quickly how to navigate effectively around their cribs.

Helping your baby sleep through the night is also about ensuring that your baby is safe while in her crib. When you put her to bed, make sure that everything around her is safe and comfortable, and you will be able to sleep better knowing that she is in a safe place for the night.

It will still be hard for the first little while not to go running in there to check on her and make sure that she is still breathing after a few hours, but eventually you'll be happy that she is sleeping, and you'll

Sleep Little Baby

enjoy the quiet of the night knowing that she is safe and that you are doing what is best for the both of you.

Conclusion

We all need to get quality sleep. Babies need to sleep so that their physical and brain health will properly develop and we adults need sleep so that our bodies can restore and rejuvenate.

It is true, that when you become a parent, getting quality sleep may seem almost impossible, as if sleep deprivation is a typical part of life. However, this does not have to remain true forever.

Many parents, my husband and I included, were able to get some good shut-eye through sleep training our babies— which benefitted not only our little one, but us as well.

I hope that you will use the tips and methods that you learned in this book as you coach your child to sleep. No, it will not be an easy feat, but you will get there through patience and commitment.

What's a few months of "hard" work when the result is many good nights of sleep for you and your baby?

You can do it, mom and dad!

Lastly, if you enjoyed this audiobook I ask that you please take the time to review it on Audible.com. Your honest feedback would be greatly appreciated.

Thank you.

www.ingramcontent.com/pod-product-compliance
Lightning Source LLC
Chambersburg PA
CBHW031109080526
44587CB00011B/890